THE WOOD ENGRAVINGS OF
WINSLOW HOMER

THE BATTLE OF BUNKER HILL—WATCHING THE FIGHT FROM COPP'S HILL, IN BOSTON.

THE WOOD ENGRAVINGS OF
WINSLOW HOMER

EDITED WITH AN INTRODUCTION BY

BARBARA GELMAN

BOUNTY BOOKS

A DIVISION OF CROWN PUBLISHERS, INC., NEW YORK

© 1969, BY CROWN PUBLISHERS, INC.
LIBRARY OF CONGRESS CATALOG CARD NUMBER: 73-75096
PRINTED IN THE UNITED STATES OF AMERICA
PUBLISHED SIMULTANEOUSLY IN CANADA
BY GENERAL PUBLISHING COMPANY LIMITED

Contents

c.1

Introduction

THE WOOD ENGRAVINGS OF WINSLOW HOMER
Early Years

LONG AFTER he had become a famous painter, Winslow Homer was asked to help prepare a brief autobiography for the Metropolitan Museum of Art. In it, he wrote that as a young man he had come to New York to learn to be a painter. During this period, he added almost as an afterthought, "...the young man [Homer] supported himself by doing illustrations for the popular journals of the day." With these few words, the celebrated artist dismissed a twenty-year career and the more than two hundred wood engravings that were the fruits of those years.

NOTORIOUSLY RETICENT about his life and works, Homer may be forgiven his characteristic terseness. But unfortunately—and unjustly—the world of art, until very recently, has been almost as brief about these delightful illustrations as Homer. While books of and about his paintings have abounded, with rare exception, most of the wood engravings have lain hidden in museum print rooms and private collections, inaccessible to the public at large. And yet, this enormous body of work that represents in some ways another entire career could probably shed more light on his paintings than all of the books and theories currently making the rounds. For it was Homer, popular pictorial journalist and storyteller, who ultimately gave birth to Homer, the narrative and almost brutally honest painter. And it was Homer, superb draftsman and designer for the wood block, who translated those skills into the unique painting style that made him famous.

BUT RATHER THAN DISCUSS THEM, let us look at the wood engravings. Charming, elegant, honest at a time when sentimentality was ubiquitous, they stand by themselves as separate entities, independent works of art worthy of display. At their very worst, they are delightful reminders of an age that America will never see again, brought to life by Homer's accurate eye and hand. At their best, for sheer beauty, strength, and style, they are equal to the most important of Homer's art. Indeed, there are some authorities who suggest that while Homer's paintings are tremendously popular in America, in the larger realms of art—when one considers the history of art from its beginnings—Homer is, after all, just another painter. But his wood engravings, they insist, rank among the best ever produced.

TRUE OR NOT, if one studies this collection from beginning to end, Homer's development, from a talented neophyte who might be sketching for any medium to the distinctive artist whose technique is inextricably wed to his means of visual communication, is obvious. For Homer, the medium is, indeed, a large part of the message. And the bold line, the relatively shallow perspective, the large masses and shapes that have become his artistic hallmark, all have their origins in the wood block. This is not to suggest that Homer was a slave to wood, or that he was not a free spirit artistically. In fact, quite the opposite is true. But he did know and understand the nature of wood, and he allowed its very limitations to teach him what was best. As his knowledge grew, so did his inventiveness and his particular technique. Apparently, he liked what he learned, for more than a little of the style born of that technique found its way to his paintings. There are instances in which his wood engravings and his paintings bear more than just a passing resemblance to one another in both subject matter and style, and this tells us something about Homer as a man and as an artist. For the very prudent Mr. Homer, a Yankee by birth, breeding, and nature, was never one to let anything he had ever seen, heard, or learned go to waste.

WINSLOW HOMER was born February 24, 1836, in Boston, the descendant of a long line of people who had made New England their home for more than two hundred years. When Winslow was six, his family moved to Cambridge, a town not yet taken over by that huge installation of higher education, Harvard University. His mother, born in Maine but brought up in Cambridge herself, wanted to get her boys out of the city, into the country where they would have lots of room to play. They loved it, and if the most persistent motifs in Homer's art are any indication, the appeal of the country was never forgotten.

THOUGH NOT A PARTICULARLY outstanding student, or even a very spectacular boy, Homer did show a very early penchant for sketching. It is surprising, on the one hand, that Winslow should have been encouraged in this direction as much as he was. This was Victorian, staid New England, where boys were not exactly pushed into a life of art, unless it was the literary variety. The visual arts were considered a cultural backwash. But Winslow's mother, whom he adored, was an amateur painter of no mean talent. She was, no doubt, his first and constant inspiration.

HIS FATHER, Charles Savage Homer, was a hardware importer and, one would think, of a more practical bent. But he also encouraged his young son's talent, and from his constant travels (another proclivity Homer would later inherit), he sent back prints and sketch books for Winslow to study and copy. It was his father who finally pushed Homer into the professional world of art.

NO LESS SUPPORT AND SYMPATHY came from his brothers, Charles and Arthur, who remained his best friends for a lifetime.

SUCH ARE THE FACTS of his early life as they might have been divulged by the secretive Mr. Homer, who once claimed that the appearance of a biography which plumed the personal aspects of his life "would kill me." But even from such a brief account, there emerges the picture of a very warm, giving family, and an immensely happy childhood. In fact, so happy was his childhood that, according to Homer himself and those who knew him best, he was rather loath to leave it for many, many years. But in 1855, at age nineteen and with no college prospects in view, Homer was forced to think about the adult business of earning a living. At this point, despite all of the encouragement his family had given him, nobody, including Homer, seriously considered the possibility that he might become an artist. The elder Homer, however, while reading his morning newspaper, fastened upon a help-wanted ad that he thought might be just the thing for Winslow. It seemed that Bufford Lithographers, in Cambridge, was looking for "a boy with a taste for drawing. No other wanted." The elder Homer not only encouraged Winslow to try for the job, but, as an acquaintance of Bufford (they served in the same volunteer fire department), he actively helped him to secure it. It was an apprenticeship, and the paternal Homer had to pay $300 to ensure Winslow the position. But pay he did, although Winslow did such a good job that a great deal of the money was duly refunded.

IT WAS APPARENT from the beginning that Winslow's talent was superior. While the other apprentices got the routine and rather dull tasks, Homer was quickly put to work drawing and designing. His first job was to design the title pages for some sheet music, ordered by Oliver Ditson of Boston. "Katy Darling" and "Oh, Whistle, and I'll Come to You, My Lad" were two of his earliest assignments.

BUT IN SPITE OF EARLY SUCCESS and much praise, Homer bitterly resented working while the other boys, as he put it, were out enjoying life. And as soon as he had completed his two-year tour of duty, Homer lifted his head from the lithographer's stone—for him an intolerable grindstone—and made his way to Boston to pursue a life of art according to his own tastes. Never again would he allow himself to be trapped by a steady, conventional job.

THE ILLUSTRATED WEEKLY AND WOOD ENGRAVING
Homer's Introduction to the World of Art

IN 1857, TWENTY-ONE-YEAR-OLD Winslow Homer arrived in Boston. A brand-new venture had recently burst onto the publishing scene: the illustrated weekly, a medium as startling and revolutionary in its day as electronic communications has been in ours. Because the illustrated weeklies, a cross between contemporary magazines and pictorial newspapers, could be gotten out quickly, with pictures, and at a reasonable price, they were an immediate success.

UNTIL THEN, text could be printed quickly and inexpensively, but illustrations, reproduced by time-consuming engraving methods, were very costly. To be sure, there were many prints, illustrated books, and magazines, and the public loved them. But because of slow production, they had to be planned far in advance of their sale date, and they were not cheap. They lacked the timeliness of a newspaper or even of a contemporary monthly magazine, and their high cost restricted the number of copies sold.

WHAT WAS NEEDED was a new, fast, and cheap way to reproduce pictures in great quantity. What actually happened was the rediscovery, with some added refinements, of what may be man's oldest way of printing both words and pictures—the woodcut.

BLOCK BOOKS, so called since they were made up of a series of reproduced woodcuts, were printed long before the *Gutenberg Bible.* Well known in Europe, the nature of the woodcut itself made them relatively easy to produce. To execute one, a draftsman simply drew the object he wanted to reproduce on a block of wood. Then an engraver would carve away all of the blank spots, leaving the picture in relief. The block was coated with ink, and the relief image was stamped out on paper much in the same way that type is. This was much easier than intricate engraving, intaglio style, on stone and metal—but much more limited.

THE VERY QUALITY that makes wood easy to carve, its softness and flexibility, also makes it a medium of transfer that lacks durability. It does not take very long for the impression to wear away. And, except in the hands of master draftsmen and engravers expert in the craft, the artist was limited in his accomplishments. Lines had to be thick, lest they be destroyed in the carving, and the flat, black line characteristic of the wood engraving had none of the refinement we would later come to associate with lithographs and etchings. Even the best artists, recognizing the limitations of the wood, generally tried for a rough-hewn kind of intimacy, which even today remains the wood block's chief contribution to art. Except for the extraordinary artist and carver, most would-be publishers and illustrators had to be content with some charming but primitive and stylized work.

BUT IN THE SECOND HALF of the nineteenth century, shortly before Homer's arrival in Boston, it was discovered that if one drew and engraved on very fine-grained boxwood, that had been polished and coated white until it had a paper-like smoothness, a finer, freer, more natural line could be carved out than had ever been possible before. Add to this a process that transferred the wood engraving to a metal plate so that a huge number of prints could be reproduced mechanically, and here was the quick, inexpensive method of printing illustrations so desperately sought after.

WELL, ALMOST. There were still the badly needed illustrators, of course, and—more important at this stage of the game—expert engravers to transfer those illustrations onto the reproducible wood engravings.

Wood engravers were rare in this country because the medium had never been popular. But with the pictorial-weekly boom, scores of young, talented engravers from France, where wood engraving had long been practiced, flocked to America in search of work. One of these young Frenchmen, newly arrived in Boston and working for *Ballou's Pictorial Drawing-Room Companion,* introduced Homer to the wood block.

SOON AFTERWARD, young Winslow tried his hand at sketching for the block and sold his first illustration to *Ballou's,* a somewhat stuffy Boston weekly. A bit later, he began to appear in New York's smart, chic *Harper's Weekly.* Winslow Homer, in less than a month's time after his arrival in Boston, had become a professional free-lance illustrator.

HOMER'S EARLIEST ILLUSTRATIONS have been described as rather undistinguished pieces of commercial art which might have been done by any competent young hack. Certainly, they are not the ultimate Homer. Overdetailed, crowded, filled with cross-hatching and other complex lines that added unnecessary tone or depth to lilies which did not need the gilding, the engravings nonetheless still have a style that is somehow special. Elegant, charming, and utterly decorative at their best, they indicate a way of life and the kind of beauty—especially feminine beauty—that existed at the time. Perhaps it is this elegance, especially of the female, that best characterizes Homer's early work. Indeed, there are some who give him credit for inventing the American Girl, with her hoop skirts, elaborate costumes and frills that Winslow so obviously loved to draw. His gentlemen, like the young Homer himself, were very proper and a bit dandyish in dress. And like Homer, they spent most of their free time very wisely—out in country resorts with lovely girls. (See "May Day in the Country," for the best example of Homer's grace, delicacy, and elegance, at this time.)

EVEN AT THIS EARLY STAGE of his career, Homer loved drawing rural scenes, both the manicured countryside of the resort, and the simple, charming, homespun of real farmers and country folk. When he was free to execute this type of sketch, he was at his best. "Husking the Corn in New England," "Picnicking in the Country," and "The Dance After the Husking" all have a kind of lightness, charm, and grace that would be missing from his later work.

STILL, A YOUNG ILLUSTRATOR cannot always draw what he likes, and Homer sometimes received "assignments" that did not please him. This is especially true of his earliest material for *Ballou's,* where he was frequently called upon to execute portraits, taken from photographs, of persons who are now, for the most part, obscure. Some are included in this collection because they are representative of a certain stage of his work. However, most have been eliminated in favor of the Boston street scenes and the marvelous rustic views which appeared in both *Ballou's* and *Harper's Weekly*. In the latter illustrations he was allowed that freedom and independence which was to become so necessary to him for as long as he lived. In this sense, it might be said that Homer never really was the conventional illustrator. Specific assignments were few, and like the painter and fine artist, he was generally allowed to draw what he liked.

IN 1859, BALLOU'S WENT OUT OF BUSINESS, and Homer, as much to be near his prime source of income *(Harper's Weekly)*, as to "learn to be a painter," moved to New York. His work changed very little until the beginning of the Civil War, and he did not start painting in earnest for another four years.

THE CIVIL WAR YEARS
Winslow Homer, Journalist

WHEN HOMER ARRIVED IN NEW YORK, *Harper's Weekly* offered him a permanent job as a staff illustrator, but the "bondage" he had suffered at Bufford's was still too fresh and painful in his memory. He refused. However, two years later, at the outbreak of the Civil War, *Harper's* did hire him as a full-time picture correspondent, both in Washington and at the front. This was the only commitment of any duration that Homer was ever to make again (although he did waiver once, shortly after this period). Exactly how long he remained at the front is unknown, but we do know that his stay was short.

NEVERTHELESS, this assignment proved to be great training for his camera eye, and, as witnessed by his illustrations, Homer did, indeed, see a lot. Battles were grim and brutal, not glorious heroic charges, and Homer rendered them as such. War was frequently boring or poised waiting, rather than continuous action, and Homer saw that and drew it. Armies were made of disorganized, raggie-taggle groups of men, not handsomely dressed, parading regiments, and this too the artist noted. It was perhaps the accepted, everyday brutality of war that affected Homer's style most strongly. Although some of his earliest war illustrations suffered, because they were sent back as sketches for other artists to draw on the block of wood, one can still see an evolution taking place in Homer's whole artistic

point of view. From early panorama, the illustrations become simpler in their rendering and more concentrated in their subject matter. From the crowded "A Bayonet Charge," the magnificently designed, almost starkly simple "A Sharp-Shooter on Picket Duty" was a long step artistically. (This was also one of Homer's earliest paintings.)

YET THE ACTUAL WAR SCENES, although their influence was great, did not interest Homer most. The behind-the-lines waiting—soldiers getting paid and running to the suttler's (supply) tent for their herrings and drink, amusing themselves during the war's long intervals, squabbling, waiting for letters and packages from home, celebrating holidays without loved ones—in short, the human, ordinary everydayness of war fascinated him, as everyday events always did in every area of life. And he rendered behind-the-lines and battle scenes alike without the detailed "prettiness" which had characterized his earlier work. (However, because Homer's talents as a decorative designer were great, some of that "prettiness" would never totally disappear.) Here, instead of brutality, was humor, but of the gentle, honest sort that never caricatured or made people more—or less— than they really were.

LONG BEFORE THE WAR'S END, however, the quiet, dapper Winslow Homer was back among his elegant ladies, whose very beauty was a boon to the war effort, and his dignified gentlemen, some of them in uniform now. During this period, or so some vague rumors have it, Homer actually fell in love with one of his charming women. But no marriage resulted, and Homer never fell in love again. Despite his obvious response to feminine beauty, Homer never did marry, and so the story may be true.

BUT HOMER HAD OTHER THINGS to think about at this point. Six years after his entry into the art world, he had begun to paint. Within three years, he began to receive recognition for these efforts, and he planned a trip to that mecca for all artists—Paris. Shortly after the war's end, in 1866, Homer embarked on his journey, remaining in Paris for a year.

THE WAR'S END
Paris and the Years After

ONE OR ANOTHER of four theories, separately and in combination, have persisted to explain the influences on Homer's art. He was entirely self-taught; he learned from British magazine illustrators like Millais; Japanese prints, which became known to the Western art world shortly before Homer came on the scene, profoundly influenced him; and, finally, he was supposed to have followed the nineteenth-century French Impressionists.

ALL FOUR THEORIES have some basis in fact. In the formal, academic sense at least, Homer had no art training; some of his illustrations do bear a striking resemblance to Millais' work; there is ample evidence that he admired many Japanese prints, both at home and abroad, and many of the illustrations in this volume have the same simplicity, the near-flat asymmetrical decorative quality one associates with oriental prints; even though Homer came long before any but the earliest and most tentative thrusts of Impressionism, he may well have been a natural impressionist himself.

STILL, NONE OF THESE THEORIES has ever been able to explain, in terms of his art, just exactly what happened to Homer during his year in Paris and the French countryside. Supporters of the first two theories say absolutely nothing happened. Indeed, it is true that only two Homer illustrations were published during that year, 1866. Yet there can be little doubt that he loved France. He did, after all, remain the year. Once, when he had run out of money, he wrote home to a friend, begging him to sell some paintings he had left if only for the worth of the frames, so that he might continue his stay.

THE LATTER HYPOTHESES do not explain too much either. As mentioned above, Homer was too early to have seen any real examples of Impressionism. He may have seen his first Japanese prints at this time (there was a great art exposition in Paris at which the prints played a major role), but there was so much more to see in the art capital of the world that there was more likely a cumulative effect.

IF THE ARTIST in question were anybody but Homer, this might be explanation enough. The fact is, though, that Homer disliked museums and expositions, and felt it was futile, even harmful, to look at too much art, especially somebody else's. As for the Japanese-print theory, the prints had already made their appearance in America, and it seems more than likely that he had seen them before his trip abroad. However, they did cause a sensation in Paris that year, and Homer may have been impressed. In any event, whatever he saw in Paris had been seen briefly, for soon after his arrival, he left for the country, where he spent most of his time in the company of few, if any, artists.

VERY LITTLE ELSE IS KNOWN about Homer's trip—especially what he may have learned in terms of art. Nevertheless, when he returned, in 1867, it was obvious that something important had happened. Never before had his lines been so strong, his draftsmanship so good, or his style more distinctive. It was as though every seed of uniqueness and talent had come to fruition. Extraneous detail would almost give way entirely to boldness and simplicity; single incidents and central characters (fewer than he had used before) would become more important, as grand-vista backgrounds faded to no more than necessary suggestion. Homer was "focusing-in," giving up the long shot for the close-up, the self-conscious spectacle for the nearly unconscious, intimate drama that means the name Homer to all familiar with his art. His design, in the manner of the Japanese prints, was becoming more and more asymmetrical, and yet the balance he achieved was supremely pleasing to the eye (see "Homeward-Bound"). In Homer's day, when balance, design, and symmetry all meant pretty much the same thing, this was no small or ordinary achievement.

WHILE HOMER'S TECHNIQUE seemed to have undergone some kind of revolution, his subject matter had not. Sea and beach scenes, ice-skating tableaus, views of rural life, both farm and resort, still caught his eye, as did pretty girls, whether in elegant or simple country dress. But what a difference in interpretation. Large, bold figures and shapes dominate, where once the artist had lost himself in crowds and a myriad of action and detail; his skies and his waterways, once filled with diagonal lines to denote tone, now become the blotty-looking, washy drawings we identify with him. Certainly, some of his loveliest and best works in any medium appeared during this period: "Chestnutting," "A Winter-Morning—Shovelling Out," "The Fishing Party," "The Dinner Horn," to name but a few. Some are studies for, or later interpretations (by the artist himself) of, his paintings, and they fare very well by comparison. And although most experts feel that he had not yet reached the height of his powers as an illustrator, there are some wood engravings during this period that are unequaled for spontaneity, extraordinary beauty, and simplicity by anything Homer has ever done. Though not so "finished" or polished as the later illustrations, their intimacy and design frequently make them more nearly what a wood engraving should be.

BY THIS TIME, HOMER was working for any periodical. *Harper's Bazaar,* *Appleton's Journal of Literature, Science and Art, Every Saturday,* and his old standby *Harper's Weekly* were among the better known of his clients. All knew his work and were content to let him sketch freely whatever pleased him, the kind of situation Homer loved best. He did do some story illustrations (assignments based strictly on prewritten text) for a periodical called *Galaxy*. These, together with a few city scenes (he had almost entirely moved away from doing any city sketches), are nearly unrecognizable as Homer's work: They lack all of his exceptional qualities. But we include them, not only for the sake of being as complete as possible, but because they point out, better than anything else, Homer's ability to work really well when he was truly free from outside direction. As suggested earlier, in this sense, he was always more painter than he was the conventional illustrator. In just about any artistic situation, Homer was certainly adequate. But only when he was totally independent —a situation he managed to maintain most of his life—was he superb.

THE RISE AND FALL OF AN ILLUSTRATOR
1873–1875

NEITHER CRITICS nor those who value fine work can ignore the wood engravings that Homer produced in 1873 and 1874. These are the greats, the culmination of nearly twenty years of draftsmanship and designing for the wood block. In his own singular way and style, Homer had achieved a nearly perfect union with his medium.

MEANWHILE HOMER was going on with his painting. "Snap-the-Whip," "The Noon Recess," "See-Saw," "Gloucester, Massachusetts," and "Sea-Side Sketches—A Clam-Bake" are only a few of the famous illustrations Homer did in oils and watercolors (a new medium for him at this point).

Yet, somewhat altered, but totally recognizable, many of the wood engravings are even better than their "fine-art" counterparts. The most obvious example is "Snap-the-Whip": Compare the wood engraving with the painting and you will see that the wood engraving is a far more finished, and even more interesting, work of art. In this period, many of the illustrations surpass the paintings in a variety of ways.

EVEN MORE INTERESTING than a quality comparison between wood engravings and paintings is a style comparison. While the technical emphasis in a sketch for a wood engraving differs markedly from that used in a painting, the style born of the former—the large masses and shapes, the absence of too much detail, the relatively shallow perspective, the asymmetrical decorative quality—all became important ingredients in Homer's paintings. Homer's objective camera eye never failed him, providing the paradoxical, close-up intimacy which has always characterized the best of all wood engravings.

IN 1875 HOMER did very few illustrations, and those few were far below his usual standard. In fact, they were just plain bad. Had Homer lost his genius? Later some sporadic but good illustrations belied this conclusion. But Homer had found a new love, watercolors, and he left the world of illustration to devote himself entirely to that medium.

PAINTING'S GAIN was certainly illustration's loss, and yet the lessons taught him by that first and most influential teacher, the wood block, never did leave him. Basically, in terms of the narrative and representational quality of his art, he always remained an illustrator. And his bold, and in his time revolutionary, style was always wed to the wood engraving.

CAPTAIN J. W. WATKINS.

CORNER OF WINTER, WASHINGTON AND SUMMER STREETS, BOSTON.

THE MATCH BETWEEN THE SOPHS AND FRESHMEN—THE OPENING.

FRESHMEN.   SOPHS.   JUNIORS.   SENIORS.

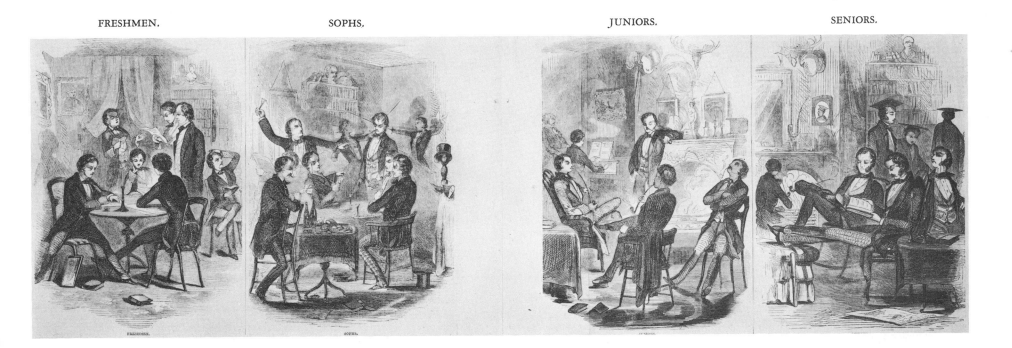

A BOSTON WATERING-CART

VIEW IN SOUTH MARKET STREET, BOSTON.

REMBRANDT PEALE.

EMIGRANT ARRIVAL AT CONSTITUTION WHARF, BOSTON.

7

BOSTON EVENING STREET SCENE, AT THE CORNER OF COURT AND BRATTLE STREETS.

THE "COLD TERM," BOSTON—SCENE, CORNER OF MILK AND WASHINGTON STREETS.

SPRING IN THE CITY.

THE BOSTON COMMON.

CLASS DAY, AT HARVARD UNIVERSITY, CAMBRIDGE, MASSACHUSETTS.

12

THE BATHE AT NEWPORT.

13

PICNICKING IN THE WOODS.

HUSKING THE CORN IN NEW ENGLAND.

DRIVING HOME THE CORN.

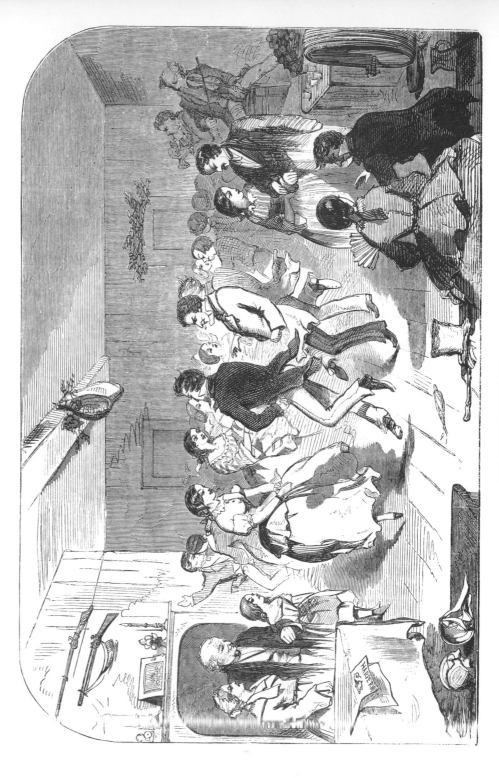

THE DANCE AFTER THE HUSKING.

THANKSGIVING DAY—WAYS AND MEANS.

17

THANKSGIVING DAY—ARRIVAL AT THE OLD HOME.

THANKSGIVING DAY—THE DINNER.

19

THANKSGIVING DAY—THE DANCE.

CHRISTMAS—GATHERING EVERGREENS.

21

THE CHRISTMAS-TREE.

CHRISTMAS OUT OF DOORS.

SANTA CLAUS AND HIS PRESENTS.

SLEIGHING IN HAYMARKET SQUARE, BOSTON.

SKATING AT BOSTON.

LA PETITE ANGELINA AND MISS C. THOMPSON, AT THE BOSTON MUSEUM.

EVENING SCENE AT THE SKATING PARK, BOSTON.

MARCH WINDS.

APRIL SHOWERS.

THE NEW TOWN OF BELMONT, MASSACHUSETTS.

MAY-DAY IN THE COUNTRY.

CRICKET PLAYERS ON BOSTON COMMON.

MADAME LABORDE, THE PRIMA DONNA.

AUGUST IN THE COUNTRY—THE SEA-SHORE.

A CADET HOP AT WEST POINT.

FALL GAMES—THE APPLE-BEE

36

A MERRY CHRISTMAS AND A HAPPY NEW YEAR.

THE SLEIGHING SEASON. — THE UPSET

A SNOW SLIDE IN THE CITY.

39

The Parsonage.

BY ELLA RODMAN.

THE BUDS.

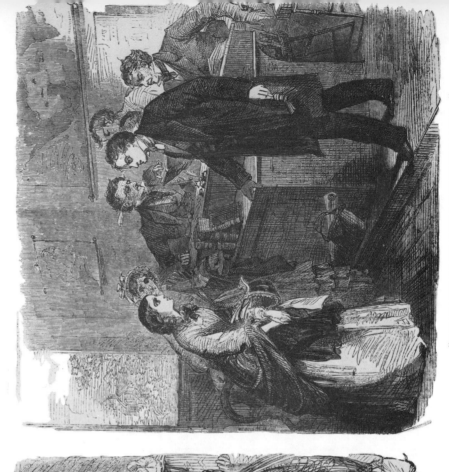

"ALLOW ME TO EXAMINE THE YOUNG LADY—"

THE MEETING AFTER THE MARRIAGE.

40

ON THE BEACH.

MEADOWBROOK PARSONAGE.

THE LADY IN BLACK.

MRS. OTCHESON AT THE PIANO.

SKATING ON THE LADIES' SKATING-POND IN THE CENTRAL PARK, NEW YORK.

HON. J. L. M. CURRY, OF ALABAMA.

SCENE IN UNION SQUARE, NEW YORK, ON A MARCH DAY.

CHIME OF THIRTEEN BELLS FOR CHRIST CHURCH, CAMBRIDGE, MASSACHUSETTS, MANUFACTURED BY MESSRS. HENRY N. HOOPER & CO., OF BOSTON.

THE DRIVE IN THE CENTRAL PARK, NEW YORK, SEPTEMBER, 1860.

THANKSGIVING DAY, 1860—THE TWO GREAT CLASSES OF SOCIETY.

HON. ABRAHAM LINCOLN, BORN IN KENTUCKY, FEBRUARY 12, 1809.

EXPULSION OF NEGROES AND ABOLITIONISTS FROM TREMONT TEMPLE, BOSTON, MASSACHUSETTS, ON DECEMBER 3, 1860.

49

THE GEORGIA DELEGATION IN CONGRESS.

UNDERWOOD. CRAWFORD. HARDEMAN. TOOMES. LOVE. JONES. IVERSON. HILL. GARTRELL. JACKSON.

THE SECEDING MISSISSIPPI DELEGATION
IN CONGRESS.

51

REUBEN DAVIS.
LUCIUS Q. C. LAMAR.

SENATOR JEFFERSON DAVIS.
SENATOR ALBERT G. BROWN.
WILLIAM BARKSDALE.

OTHO R. SINGLETON.
JOHN J. M'RAE.

THE SECEDING SOUTH CAROLINA DELEGATION.

KEITT.
BOYCE.

CHESNUT.

M'QUEEN.
ASHMORE.

HAMMOND.

BONHAM.
MILES.

SEEING THE OLD YEAR OUT.

53

THE INAUGURAL PROCESSION AT WASHINGTON PASSING THE GATE OF THE CAPITOL GROUNDS.

PRESIDENTS BUCHANAN AND LINCOLN ENTERING THE SENATE CHAMBER BEFORE THE INAUGURATION.

THE INAUGURATION OF ABRAHAM LINCOLN AS PRESIDENT OF THE UNITED STATES, AT THE CAPITOL, WASHINGTON, MARCH 4, 1861.

GENERAL THOMAS SWEARING IN THE VOLUNTEERS CALLED INTO THE SERVICE OF THE UNITED STATES AT WASHINGTON, D.C.

THE SEVENTY-NINTH REGIMENT (HIGHLANDERS), NEW YORK STATE MILITIA.

THE ADVANCED GUARD OF THE GRAND ARMY OF THE UNITED STATES CROSSING THE LONG BRIDGE OVER THE POTOMAC AT 2 A.M. ON MAY 24, 1861.

THE WAR-MAKING HAVELOCKS FOR THE VOLUNTEERS.

CREW OF THE UNITED STATES STEAM-SLOOP "COLORADO," SHIPPED AT BOSTON, JUNE, 1861.

FILLING CARTRIDGES AT THE UNITED STATES ARSENAL, AT WATERTOWN, MASSACHUSETTS.

Courtesy of The Metropolitan Museum of Art, New York City, Harris Brisbane Dick Fund, 1929

THE SONGS OF THE WAR.

A BIVOUAC FIRE ON THE POTOMAC.

GREAT FAIR GIVEN AT THE CITY ASSEMBLY ROOMS, NEW YORK, DECEMBER, 1861, IN AID OF THE CITY POOR.

CHRISTMAS BOXES IN CAMP—CHRISTMAS, 1861.

THE SKATING SEASON—1862.

Rebel works seen from Gen.l Porters Division.

Reconnoissance in force by Gen.l Gorman

Assault on Rebel batt.y at Lee's Mills by 3.d Vermont Volunteers.

The enemy's works near Yorktown

The Ocean Queen conveying troops to Yorktown

OUR ARMY BEFORE YORKTOWN, VIRGINIA.

THE UNION CAVALRY AND ARTILLERY STARTING IN PURSUIT OF THE REBELS UP THE YORKTOWN TURNPIKE.

REBELS OUTSIDE THEIR WORKS AT YORKTOWN RECONNOITRING [sic] WITH DARK LANTERNS.

CHARGE OF THE FIRST MASSACHUSETTS REGIMENT ON A REBEL RIFLE PIT NEAR YORKTOWN.

THE ARMY OF THE POTOMAC—OUR OUTLYING PICKET IN THE WOODS.

NEWS FROM THE WAR.

THE WAR FOR THE UNION, 1862—A CAVALRY CHARGE.

THE SURGEON AT WORK AT THE REAR DURING AN ENGAGEMENT.

THE WAR FOR THE UNION, 1862—A BAYONET CHARGE.

THE INFLUENCE OF WOMAN

THE SISTER OF CHARITY

HOME TIDINGS

OUR WOMEN AND THE WAR.

THE ARMY OF THE POTOMAC—A SHARP-SHOOTER ON PICKET DUTY.

THANKSGIVING IN CAMP.

A SHELL IN THE REBEL TRENCHES.

WINTER-QUARTERS IN CAMP—THE INSIDE OF A HUT.

PAY-DAY IN THE ARMY OF THE POTOMAC

HOME FROM THE WAR.

THE APPROACH OF THE BRITISH PIRATE "ALABAMA."

84

THE RUSSIAN BALL—IN THE SUPPER-ROOM.

85

THE GREAT RUSSIAN BALL AT THE ACADEMY OF MUSIC, NOVEMBER 5, 1863.

HALT OF A WAGON TRAIN.

"ANY THING FOR ME, IF YOU PLEASE?"—POST-OFFICE OF THE BROOKLYN FAIR
IN AID OF THE SANITARY COMMISSION.

FLORAL DEPARTMENT OF THE GREAT FAIR.

ARMY OF THE POTOMAC—SLEEPING ON THEIR ARMS.

THANKSGIVING-DAY IN THE ARMY—AFTER DINNER: THE WISH-BONE.

HOLIDAY IN CAMP—SOLDIERS PLAYING "FOOT-BALL."

OUR WATERING-PLACES—THE EMPTY SLEEVE AT NEWPORT.

OUR WATERING-PLACES—HORSE-RACING AT SARATOGA.

THANKSGIVING DAY—HANGING UP THE MUSKET.

THANKSGIVING DAY—THE CHURCH PORCH.

96

THE VETERAN IN A NEW FIELD.

THE BRIGHT SIDE.

THE BIRD-CATCHERS.

SWINGING ON A BIRCH TREE.

THE MIDNIGHT COAST.

JOHN ANDREW

99

A PARISIAN BALL — DANCING AT THE MABILLE, PARIS

A PARISIAN BALL—DANCING AT THE CASINO.

HOMEWARD-BOUND.

ART-STUDENTS AND COPYISTS IN THE LOUVRE GALLERY, PARIS.

ST. VALENTINE'S DAY—THE OLD STORY IN ALL LANDS.

OPENING DAY IN NEW YORK.

Courtesy of The Metropolitan Museum of Art, New York City. Harris Brisbane Dick Fund, 1933

"SHE TURNED HER FACE TO THE WINDOW."

"YOU ARE REALLY PICTURESQUE, MY LOVE."

WATCHING THE CROWS.

THE FOURTH OF JULY IN TOMPKINS SQUARE, NEW YORK—"THE SOGERS
ARE COMING!"

FIRE-WORKS ON THE NIGHT OF THE FOURTH OF JULY.

NEW ENGLAND FACTORY LIFE—"BELL-TIME."

Courtesy of The New-York Historical Society, New York City

FATIMA ENTERS THE FORBIDDEN CLOSET.

WHAT SHE SEES THERE.

DISPOSITION OF THE BODIES (INVISIBLE TO THE SPECTATORS).

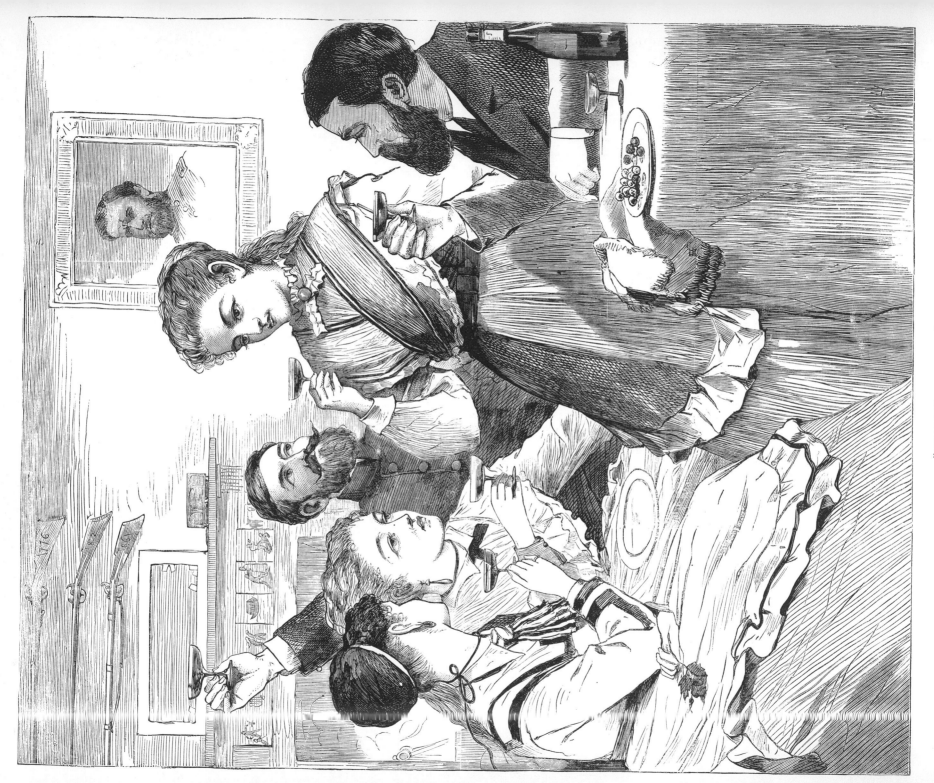

"OUR NEXT PRESIDENT."

WAITING FOR CALLS ON NEW-YEAR'S DAY.

CHRISTMAS BELLES.

THE NEW YEAR—1869.

WINTER AT SEA—TAKING IN SAIL OFF THE COAST.

Courtesy of The New-York Historical Society, New York City

JURORS LISTENING TO COUNSEL, SUPREME COURT, NEW CITY HALL, NEW YORK.

"HI! H-O-O-O! HE DONE COME. JUMBOLORO TELL YOU FUST."

120

"ALL IN THE GAY AND GOLDEN WEATHER."

THE ARTIST IN THE COUNTRY.

122

SUMMER IN THE COUNTRY.

ON THE ROAD TO LAKE GEORGE.

WHAT SHALL WE DO NEXT?

THE LAST LOAD.

THE PICNIC EXCURSION.

THE BEACH AT LONG BRANCH.

AT THE SPRING: SARATOGA.

*Courtesy of The Metropolitan
Museum of Art, New York City.
Harris Brisbane Dick Fund, 1933*

"COME!"

THE STRAW RIDE.

"I CALL THEM MY CHILDREN—TO MYSELF, SUSAN."

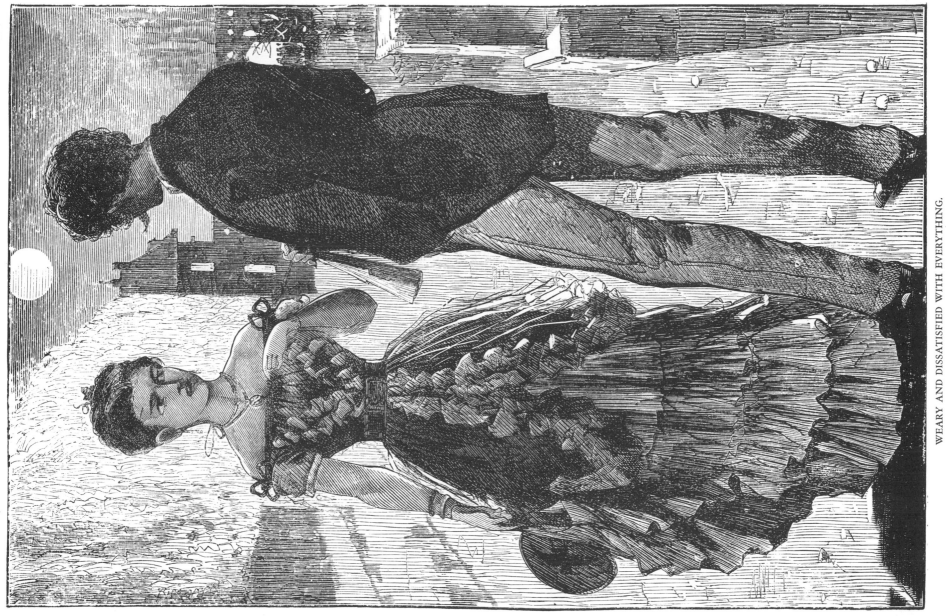

WEARY AND DISSATISFIED WITH EVERYTHING.

THE FISHING PARTY.

THE PLAYMATES.

IN CAME A STORM OF WIND, RAIN AND SPRAY—AND PORTIA.

GEORGE BLAKE'S LETTER.

137

RING OUT A SLOWLY DYING CAUSE,
AND ANCIENT FORMS OF PARTY STRIFE;
RING IN THE NOBLER MODES OF LIFE,
WITH SWEETER MANNERS, PURER LAWS.

RING OUT FALSE PRIDE IN PLACE AND BLOOD,
THE CIVIC SLANDER AND THE SPITE;
RING IN THE LOVE OF TRUTH AND RIGHT,
RING IN THE COMMON LOVE OF GOOD.

1860—1870

TENTH COMMANDMENT.

WINSLOW HOMER.

TENTH COMMANDMENT

HAVE MERCY UPON US AND INCLINE OUR HEARTS TO KEEP THIS LAW.

DANGER AHEAD.

SPRING FARM WORK—GRAFTING.

SPRING BLOSSOMS.

A QUIET DAY IN THE WOODS.

THE COOLEST SPOT IN NEW ENGLAND—SUMMIT OF MOUNT WASHINGTON.

HIGH TIDE.

LOW TIDE.

ON THE BLUFF AT LONG BRANCH, AT THE BATHING HOUR.

THE ROBIN'S NOTE

149

CHESTNUTTING.

TRAPPING IN THE ADIRONDACKS.

A WINTER-MORNING—SHOVELLING OUT.

DEER-STALKING IN THE ADIRONDACKS IN WINTER.

153

LUMBERING IN WINTER.

A COUNTRY STORE—GETTING WEIGHED.

155

CUTTING A FIGURE.

AT SEA—SIGNALLING A PASSING STEAMER.

BATHING AT LONG BRANCH—"OH, AIN'T IT COLD!"

159

MAKING HAY.

ON THE BEACH—TWO ARE COMPANY, THREE ARE NONE.

UNDER THE FALLS, CATSKILL MOUNTAINS.

THE WRECK OF THE "ATLANTIC"—CAST UP BY THE SEA.

THE NOON RECESS

THE BATHERS.

THE NOONING.

SEA-SIDE SKETCHES—A CLAM-BAKE.

"SNAP-THE-WHIP."

GLOUCESTER HARBOR.

SHIP-BUILDING, GLOUCESTER HARBOR.

"DAD'S COMING!"

171

THE LAST DAYS OF HARVEST.

THE MORNING BELL.

STATION-HOUSE LODGERS.

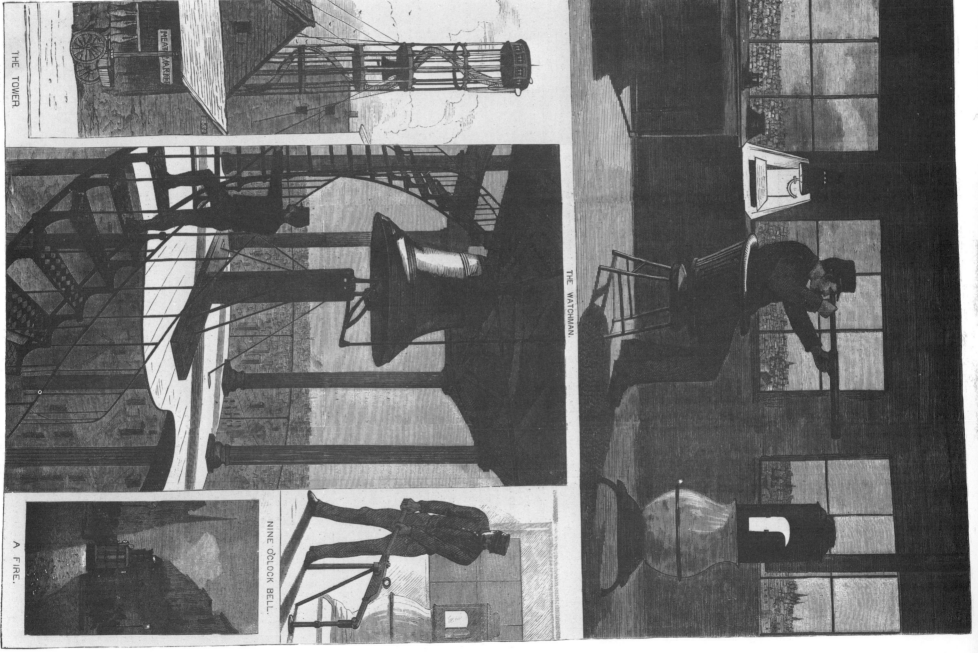

THE TOWER.

THE WATCHMAN.

A FIRE.

NINE O'CLOCK BELL.

WATCH-TOWER, CORNER OF SPRING AND VARICK STREETS, NEW YORK.

THE CHINESE IN NEW YORK.—SCENE IN A BAXTER STREET CLUB-HOUSE.

NEW YORK CHARITIES—ST. BARNABAS HOUSE, 304 MULBERRY STREET.

177

RAID ON A SAND-SWALLOW COLONY—"HOW MANY EGGS?"

GATHERING BERRIES.

ON THE BEACH AT LONG BRANCH—THE CHILDREN'S HOUR.

WAITING FOR A BITE.

SEE SAW—GLOUCESTER MASSACHUSETTS.

FLIRTING ON THE SEA-SHORE AND ON THE MEADOW.

CAMPING OUT IN THE ADIRONDACK MOUNTAINS.

THE FAMILY RECORD.

BOB: "HALLO! WHAT'S UP NOW? ARE YOUR BABIES IN HERE?"

A CHARCOAL SKETCH.

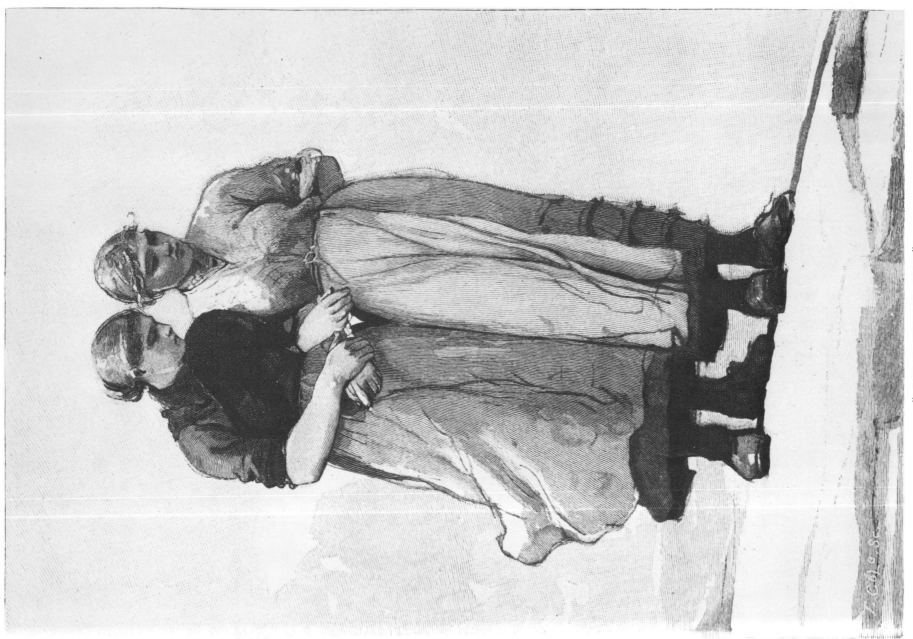

"LOOKING OVER THE CLIFF."

LISTENING TO THE VOICE FROM THE CLIFFS.

"INSIDE THE BAR."

RUSH'S LANCERS, FRANKLIN'S ADVANCE SCOUTS.

A GROUP OF PALMS.

GROWING HEMP.

192

ON ABACO ISLAND.

THE FLOWER-SELLER.

CONCH DIVERS.

SHARK-FISHING—NASSAU BAR.

TWO OF SHERIDAN'S SCOUTS.

THE BAGGAGE GUARD.

HOMER '65

PRESIDENT LINCOLN, GENERAL GRANT, AND TAD LINCOLN AT A RAILWAY STATION.

Guide to Prices

The individual wood-engravings from *Ballou's Pictorial Drawing-Room Companion* are valued at $35 each. Though they are less appealing and not so well done as the later pictures, they are much scarcer, and hence, in some cases, bring higher prices than the better illustrations.

The *Harper's Weekly* engravings are valued at from $25 to $75. The highest prices are obtained for genre types, such as "Snap-the-Whip" and "Ship-building, Gloucester Harbor." Pictures from other journals, like *Appelton's* or *Our Young Folks,* command from $15 to $75, depending on the size, quality, and scarcity of the engravings. Some very famous illustrations—such as "The Chestnutting" and "The Robin's Note"—were done for periodicals other than *Harper's,* and sell at top prices. But primarily, these were monthlies, and the engravings tended to be smaller than the *Harper's* illustrations. Generally speaking, the *Harper's* work is the most valuable.

The Harper's Weeklies, themselves, can be purchased at moderate prices, and the lucky buyer can still find some Homers in the issues, but the supply is rapidly drying up.

It must be remembered that these values are very current. Until now, only collectors and museums have been aware of these engravings, and they are the ones who controlled the prices. But now that these delightful illustrations are more generally known, there is no doubt that the prices will begin to rise.

Bibliography

NOTE: The bibliography lists the pictures in numerical sequence, in chronological order. In the book, they do not necessarily appear in the same order because of design requirements. The bibliography lists many wood engravings not shown in the book; page numbers are given for all shown.

1. CAPTAIN J. W. WATKINS. *Ballou's Pictorial Drawing-Room Companion,* June 6, 1857, p. 364. Portrait. 4" × 4½". See page 1.
2. CORNER OF WINTER, WASHINGTON AND SUMMER STREETS, BOSTON. *Ballou's Pictorial Drawing-Room Companion,* June 13, 1857, p. 369. Street scene. 9½" × 7¼". See page 2.
3. HON. WILLIAM HAILE, GOVERNOR OF NEW HAMPSHIRE. *Ballou's Pictorial Drawing-Room Companion,* July 4, 1857, p. 12. Portrait. 3½" × 4". Not shown.
4. THE MATCH BETWEEN THE SOPHS AND FRESHMEN—THE OPENING. *Harper's Weekly,* August 1, 1857, pp. 488–489. Sport scene. 21½" × 6". See page 3.
5. FRESHMEN. *Harper's Weekly,* August 1, 1857, p. 488. Student scene. 5" × 7". See page 3.
6. SOPHS. *Harper's Weekly,* August 1, 1857, p. 488. Student scene. 5" × 7". See page 3.
7. JUNIORS. *Harper's Weekly,* August 1, 1857, p. 489. Student scene. 5" × 7". See page 3.
8. SENIORS. *Harper's Weekly,* August 1, 1857, p. 489. Student scene. 5" × 7". See page 3.
9. THE FOUNTAIN ON BOSTON COMMON. *Ballou's Pictorial Drawing-Room Companion,* August 15, 1857, p. 97. Street scene. 9½" × 7¼". Not shown.
10. A BOSTON WATERING-CART. *Ballou's Pictorial Drawing-Room Companion,* September 12, 1857, p. 161. Street scene. 9½" × 7¼". See page 4.
11. THE LATE WILLIAM WOOD. *Ballou's Pictorial Drawing-Room Companion,* September 19, 1857, p. 188. Portrait. 4" × 4½". Not shown.
12. VIEW IN SOUTH MARKET STREET, BOSTON. *Ballou's Pictorial Drawing-Room Companion,* October 3, 1857, p. 209. Street scene. 9½" × 7¼". See page 5.
13. HON. ROBERT I. BURBANK. *Ballou's Pictorial Drawing-Room Companion,* October 3, 1857, p. 220. Portrait. 4" × 4½". Not shown.
14. REMBRANDT PEALE. *Ballou's Pictorial Drawing-Room Companion,* October 17, 1857, p. 241. Portrait. 6" × 7". See page 6.
15. EMIGRANT ARRIVAL AT CONSTITUTION WHARF, BOSTON. *Ballou's Pictorial Drawing-Room Companion,* October 31, 1857, p. 273. Street scene. 9½" × 5½". See page 7.
16. BOSTON EVENING STREET SCENE, AT THE CORNER OF COURT AND BRATTLE STREETS. *Ballou's Pictorial Drawing-Room Companion,* November 7, 1857, p. 289.

Street scene. 9⅜″ × 6⅜″. See page 8.

17. BLINDMAN'S BUFF. *Ballou's Pictorial Drawing-Room Companion*, November 28, 1857, p. 344. Party scene. 7″ × 4½″. Not shown.

18. HUSKING PARTY FINDING THE RED EARS. *Ballou's Pictorial Drawing-Room Companion*, November 28, 1857, p. 344. Party scene. 9⅜″ × 6⅜″. Not shown.

19. FAMILY PARTY PLAYING AT FOX AND GEESE. *Ballou's Pictorial Drawing-Room Companion*, November 28, 1857, p. 345. Party scene. 9⅜″ × 5⅜″. Not shown.

20. COASTING OUT OF DOORS. *Ballou's Pictorial Drawing-Room Companion*, November 28, 1857, p. 345. Sport scene. 7″ × 4½″. Not shown.

21. THE "COLD TERM," BOSTON—SCENE, CORNER OF MILK AND WASHINGTON STREETS. *Ballou's Pictorial Drawing-Room Companion*, March 27, 1858, p. 193. Street scene. 9⅜″ × 6⅞″. See page 9.

22. SPRING IN THE CITY. *Harper's Weekly*, April 17, 1858, p. 248. Street scene. 13¾″ × 9⅛″. See page 10.

23. THE BOSTON COMMON. *Harper's Weekly*, May 22, 1858, p. 329. Street scene. 14″ × 9¼″. See page 11.

24. CLASS DAY, AT THE HARVARD UNIVERSITY, CAMBRIDGE, MASS. *Ballou's Pictorial Drawing-Room Companion*, July 3, 1858, p. 1. Campus scene. 9⅜″ × 5½″. See page 12.

25. CAMP MEETING SKETCHES. (A) LANDING AT THE CAPE. *Ballou's Pictorial Drawing-Room Companion*, August 21, 1858, p. 120. Women transfer from barge to carriage in midstream to be taken to shore. 9⅜″ × 5″. Not shown.

26. CAMP MEETING SKETCHES. (B) MORNING ABLUTIONS. *Ballou's Pictorial Drawing-Room Companion*, August 21, 1858, p. 120. Men wash and shave in and about tents set up for revival meeting. 9⅜″ × 5″. Not shown.

27. CAMP MEETING SKETCHES. (C) COOKING. *Ballou's Pictorial Drawing-Room Companion*, August 21, 1858, p. 121. Brick ovens and open fires are used to cook meals served to attendants, seen eating in the tents. 9⅜″ × 5″. Not shown.

28. CAMP MEETING SKETCHES. (D) THE TENT. *Ballou's Pictorial Drawing-Room Companion*, August 21, 1858, p. 121. Histrionics and prayers in one of the revival-meeting tents. 9⅜″ × 5″. Not shown.

29. THE BATHE AT NEWPORT. *Harper's Weekly*, September 4, 1858, p. 568. Beach scene. 13¾″ × 9¼″. See page 13.

30. PICNICKING IN THE WOODS. *Harper's Weekly*, September 4, 1858, p. 569. Country scene. 13¾″ × 9¼″. See page 14.

31. THEODORE PARKER. *Ballou's Pictorial Drawing-Room Companion*, November 6, 1858, p. 289. Portrait. 6″ × 8″. Not shown.

32. HUSKING THE CORN IN NEW ENGLAND. *Harper's Weekly*, November 13, 1858, p. 728. Party scene. 13⅞″ × 9¼″. See page 15.

33. DRIVING HOME THE CORN. *Harper's Weekly*, November 13, 1858, p. 729. Country scene. 9¼″ × 5⅞″. See page 16.

34. THE DANCE AFTER THE HUSKING. *Harper's Weekly*, November 13, 1858, p. 729. Party scene. 9¼″ × 6″. See page 16.

35. THANKSGIVING DAY—WAYS AND MEANS. *Harper's Weekly*, November 27, 1858, p. 760. Country scene. 9¼″ × 6⅞″. See page 17.

36. THANKSGIVING DAY—ARRIVAL AT THE OLD HOME. *Harper's Weekly*, November 27, 1858, p. 760. Country scene. 9¼″ × 6½″. See page 18.

37. THANKSGIVING DAY—THE DINNER. *Harper's Weekly*, November 27, 1858, p. 761. Party scene. 9¼″ × 6⅞″. See page 19.

38. THANKSGIVING DAY—THE DANCE. *Harper's Weekly*, November 27, 1858, p. 761. Party scene. 9¼″ × 6½″. See page 20.

39. WILLIAM E. BURTON, ESQ., COMEDIAN. *Ballou's Pictorial Drawing-Room Companion*, December 4, 1858, p. 353. Portrait. 6″ × 8″. Not shown.

40. CHRISTMAS—GATHERING EVERGREENS. *Harper's Weekly*, December 25, 1858, p. 820. Country scene. 9⅛″ × 5⅞″. See page 21.

41. THE CHRISTMAS-TREE. *Harper's Weekly*, December 25, 1858, p. 820. Party scene. 9⅛″ × 5⅞″. See page 22.

42. SANTA CLAUS AND HIS PRESENTS. *Harper's Weekly*, December 25, 1858, p. 821.

Parents filling stocking. 9⅛″ × 5¾″. See page 23.

43. CHRISTMAS OUT OF DOORS. *Harper's Weekly*, December 25, 1858, p. 821. Street scene. 9⅛″ × 6″. See page 23.

44. HENRY WADSWORTH LONGFELLOW. *Ballou's Pictorial Drawing-Room Companion*, December 25, 1858, p. 401. Portrait. 6″ × 8″. Not shown.

45. HON. STEPHEN A. DOUGLAS. *Ballou's Pictorial Drawing-Room Companion*, January 8, 1859, p. 17. Portrait. 6″ × 8″. Not shown.

46. HON. CHARLES HALE, SPEAKER OF THE HOUSE, MASSACHUSETTS LEGISLATURE. *Ballou's Pictorial Drawing-Room Companion*, January 22, 1859, p. 49. Portrait. 6″ × 8″. Not shown.

47. SKATING ON JAMAICA POND, NEAR BOSTON. *Ballou's Pictorial Drawing-Room Companion*, January 29, 1859, p. 65. Sport scene. 9½″ × 5½″. Not shown.

48. SLEIGHING IN HAYMARKET SQUARE. *Ballou's Pictorial Drawing-Room Companion*, January 29, 1859, p. 72. City scene. 9⅜″ × 5″. See page 24.

49. SLEIGHING ON THE ROAD, BRIGHTON, NEAR BOSTON. *Ballou's Pictorial Drawing-Room Companion*, January 29, 1859, p. 72. Country scene. 9⅜″ × 5″. Not shown.

50. RALPH WALDO EMERSON. *Ballou's Pictorial Drawing-Room Companion*, February 5, 1859, p. 81. Portrait. 6″ × 7½″. Not shown.

51. TROTTING ON THE MILL DAM, BOSTON. *Ballou's Pictorial Drawing-Room Companion*, February 12, 1859, p. 105. Country scene. 9½″ × 5″. Not shown.

52. MRS. CUNNINGHAM, BOSTON MUSEUM. *Ballou's Pictorial Drawing-Room Companion*, February 19, 1859, p. 120. Portrait. 4″ × 4½″. Not shown.

53. MARIA PICCOLOMINI. *Ballou's Pictorial Drawing-Room Companion*, February 26, 1859, p. 129. Portrait. 6″ × 8″. Not shown.

54. NAHUM CAPEN, ESQ., POSTMASTER OF BOSTON. *Ballou's Pictorial Drawing-Room Companion*, March 5, 1859, p. 145. Portrait. 6″ × 7½″. Not shown.

55. SKATING AT BOSTON. *Harper's Weekly*, March 12, 1859, p. 173. Winter recreation scene. 13¾″ × 9¼″. See page 25.

56. LA PETITE ANGELINA AND MISS C. THOMPSON, AT THE BOSTON MUSEUM. *Ballou's Pictorial Drawing-Room Companion*, March 12, 1859, p. 168. Child actors on stage. 6¾″ × 4½″. See page 26.

57. EVENING SCENE AT THE SKATING PARK, BOSTON. *Ballou's Pictorial Drawing-Room Companion*, March 12, 1859, p. 168. Night skating-scene. 9¼″ × 4⅞″. See page 27.

58. FLETCHER WEBSTER, ESQ., SURVEYOR OF BOSTON. *Ballou's Pictorial Drawing-Room Companion*, March 19, 1859, p. 177. Portrait. 6″ × 8″. Not shown.

59. SAMUEL MASURY, DAGUERREOTYPIST AND PHOTOGRAPHER. *Ballou's Pictorial Drawing-Room Companion*, March 26, 1859, p. 205. Portrait. 4″ × 4½″. Not shown.

60. MARCH WINDS. *Harper's Weekly*, April 2, 1859, p. 216. Seasonal street-scene. 9⅛″ × 5⅞″. See page 28.

61. APRIL SHOWERS. *Harper's Weekly*, April 2, 1859, p. 216. Seasonal street-scene. 9⅛″ × 5⅞″. See page 29.

62. HON. JAMES A. PEARCE, U. S. SENATOR FROM MARYLAND. *Ballou's Pictorial Drawing-Room Companion*, April 23, 1859, p. 257. Portrait. 6″ × 8″. Not shown.

63. THE NEW TOWN OF BELMONT, MASSACHUSETTS. *Ballou's Pictorial Drawing-Room Companion*, April 23, 1859. p. 264. Country scene. 9¼″ × 4⅞″. See page 30.

64. MAY-DAY IN THE COUNTRY. *Harper's Weekly*, April 30, 1859, p. 280. Seasonal country-scene. 13¾″ × 9⅛″. See page 31.

65. THE LATE COL. SAMUEL JAQUES. *Ballou's Pictorial Drawing-Room Companion*, May 7, 1859, p. 289. Portrait. 6″ × 6½″. Not shown.

66. THE WONDERFUL DUTTON CHILDREN. *Ballou's Pictorial Drawing-Room Companion*, May 14, 1859, p. 305. Dwarf children seen in comparison to normal child and furniture. 5″ × 6¾″. Not shown.

67. SCENE ON THE BACK BAY LANDS, BOSTON. *Ballou's Pictorial Drawing-Room Companion*, May 21, 1859, p. 328. Line-drawing of persons scavaging on landfill. 9½″ × 5″. Not shown.

68. THE AQUARIAL GARDENS, BROMFIELD STREET, BOSTON. *Ballou's Pictorial Drawing-Room Companion*, May 28, 1859, p. 335. Persons seen at early-day indoor aquarium exhibit. 9⅜″ × 6½″. Not shown.

69. CRICKET PLAYERS ON BOSTON COMMON. *Ballou's Pictorial Drawing-Room Companion,* June 4, 1859, p. 360. Sport scene. 9½" × 5½". See page 32.

70. MADAME LABORDE, THE PRIMA DONNA. *Ballou's Pictorial Drawing-Room Companion,* June 25, 1859, p. 401. Portrait. 6" × 7¾". See page 33.

71. PAUL MORPHY, THE CHESS CHAMPION. *Ballou's Pictorial Drawing-Room Companion,* July 2, 1859, p. 1. Portrait. 6" × 7½". Not shown.

72. CAMBRIDGE CATTLE MARKET. *Ballou's Pictorial Drawing-Room Companion,* July 2, 1859, p. 8. Men talking business near cattle bins and rail-loading sites. 9½" × 6". Not shown.

73. FOURTH OF JULY SCENE, ON BOSTON COMMON. *Ballou's Pictorial Drawing-Room Companion,* July 9, 1859, p. 17. Boys explode fireworks as police approach to stop them. 9½" × 5½". Not shown.

74. BOSTON STREET CHARACTERS. *Ballou's Pictorial Drawing-Room Companion,* July 9, 1859, p. 24. Montage of eleven scenes, showing types of people and activities in Boston. 9½" × 13½". Not shown.

75. CAPTAIN ROBERT B. FORBES. *Ballou's Pictorial Drawing-Room Companion,* August 20, 1859, p. 113. Portrait. 6" × 7¾". Not shown.

76. AUGUST IN THE COUNTRY—THE SEA-SHORE. *Harper's Weekly,* August 27, 1859, p. 553. View of ocean with visitors about in full dress. 13¾" × 9⅛". See page 34.

77. A CADET HOP AT WEST POINT. *Harper's Weekly,* September 3, 1859, p. 568. School-dance scene. 13⅞" × 9¼". See page 35.

78. THE GRAND REVIEW AT CAMP MASSACHUSETTS, NEAR CONCORD, SEPTEMBER 9, 1859. *Harper's Weekly,* September 24, 1859, pp. 616–617. Parade scene. 20¼" × 13⅝". Not shown.

79. FALL GAMES—THE APPLE-BEE. *Harper's Weekly,* November 26, 1859, p. 761. Party scene. 13¾" × 9⅛". See page 36.

80. HON. JOHN F. POTTER, OF WISCONSIN. *Ballou's Pictorial Drawing-Room Companion,* December 3, 1859, p. 353. Portrait. 6" × 7¾". Not shown.

81. A MERRY CHRISTMAS AND A HAPPY NEW YEAR. *Harper's Weekly,* December 24, 1859, pp. 824–825. Montage of New York City scenes at holiday time. 20" × 13¾". See page 37.

82. THE SLEIGHING SEASON—THE UPSET. *Harper's Weekly,* January 14, 1860, p. 24. Winter scene, with persons being thrown from horse-drawn sleigh. 13¾" × 9⅛". See page 38.

83. A SNOW SLIDE IN THE CITY. *Harper's Weekly,* January 14, 1860, p. 25. Winter street-scene: snow falls from roofs upon passing persons. 13¾" × 9⅛". See page 39.

84. SKATING ON THE LADIES' SKATING-POND IN THE CENTRAL PARK, NEW YORK. *Harper's Weekly,* January 28, 1860, pp. 56–57. Winter skating-scene. 20⅛" × 13¾". See page 42.

85. [NO TITLE/CAPTION.] *Harper's Weekly,* February 18, 1860, p. 97. Story illustration showing woman with bonnet posting a notice on a tree. 2¼" × 4⅛". See page 40.

86. ALLOW ME TO EXAMINE THE YOUNG LADY—" *Harper's Weekly,* February 18, 1860, p. 97. Story illustration showing a young doctor holding the hand of a lady. 4½" × 4⅜". See page 40.

87. HON. J. L. M. CURRY, OF ALABAMA. *Harper's Weekly,* February 18, 1860, p. 100. Portrait. 5⅞" × 9". See page 43.

88. THE MEETING AFTER THE MARRIAGE. *Harper's Weekly,* February 25, 1860, p. 124. Story illustration. 3½" × 4⅜". See page 40.

89. THE BUDS. *Harper's Weekly,* March 3, 1860, p. 141. Story illustration. 3½" × 4½". See page 40.

90. MRS. OTCHESON AT THE PIANO. *Harper's Weekly,* March 3, 1860, p. 141. Story illustration: woman at piano. 3½" × 4⅜". See page 41.

91. ON THE BEACH. *Harper's Weekly,* March 10, 1860, p. 157. Story illustration: young people on the beach. 3½" × 4⅜". See page 41.

92. THE LADY IN BLACK. *Harper's Weekly,* March 17, 1860, p. 164. Story illustration game as caption. 3⅜" × 4¾". See page 41.

93. MEADOWBROOK PARSONAGE. Harper's Weekly, March 17, 1860. p. 164. Story illustration: home in country setting. 3⅜" × 4½". See page 41.

94. HON. ELIHU B. WASHBURNE, OF ILLINOIS, CHAIRMAN OF THE COMMITTEE ON COMMERCE. *Harper's Weekly,* March 17, 1860, p. 172. Portrait. 5⅞" × 8½". Not shown.

95. SCENE IN UNION SQUARE, NEW YORK, ON A MARCH DAY. *Harper's Weekly,* April 7, 1860, p. 224. Cartoon by Homer on the effects of windy days. 6¾" × 4¾". See page 44.

96. CHIME OF THIRTEEN BELLS FOR CHRIST CHURCH, CAMBRIDGE, MASSACHUSETTS, MANUFACTURED BY MESSRS. HENRY N. HOOPER & CO., OF BOSTON. *Harper's Weekly,* May 26, 1860, p. 324. Chimes being installed by working crew. 9¼" × 10⅞". See page 45.

97. THE DRIVE IN THE CENTRAL PARK, NEW YORK, SEPTEMBER, 1860. *Harper's Weekly,* September 15, 1860, pp. 584–585. Busy scene of carriages and horseback riders in the park. 13¾" × 9⅛". See page 46.

98. WELCOME TO THE PRINCE OF WALES. *Harper's Weekly,* October 20, 1860, p. 657. Montage showing a lady bowling, a couple slipping on the dance floor, and females waving to the Prince as he first approaches and then leaves them. 9⅛" × 10⅝". Not shown.

99. HON. ABRAHAM LINCOLN, BORN IN KENTUCKY, FEBRUARY 12, 1809. *Harper's Weekly,* November 10, 1860, p. 705. Portrait. 9⅛" × 10¾". See page 48.

100. THANKSGIVING DAY, 1860—THE TWO GREAT CLASSES OF SOCIETY. *Harper's Weekly,* December 1, 1860, pp. 760–761. Montage drawings showing both the rich and poor classes of 1860. 20¼" × 14". See page 47.

101. HON. ROGER B. TANEY, CHIEF-JUSTICE OF THE UNITED STATES, December 8, 1860, p. 769. Portrait. 5⅝" × 8⅞". Not shown.

102. EXPULSION OF NEGROES AND ABOLITIONISTS FROM TREMONT TEMPLE, BOSTON, MASSACHUSETTS, ON DECEMBER 3, 1860. *Harper's Weekly,* December 15, 1860, p. 788. News illustration. 9¼" × 6⅞". See page 49.

103. THE SECEDING SOUTH CAROLINA DELEGATION. *Harper's Weekly,* December 22, 1860, p. 801. Montage using portraits of all members of the South Carolina delegation. 9" × 10½". See page 52.

104. THE GEORGIA DELEGATION IN CONGRESS. *Harper's Weekly,* January 5, 1861, p. 1. Montage of portraits of the Georgia delegation. 9¼" × 10¾". See page 50.

105. SEEING THE OLD YEAR OUT. *Harper's Weekly,* January 5, 1861, pp. 8–9. Montage illustration showing various ways used to see the old year out. 20¼" × 13¾". See page 53.

106. THE SECEDING MISSISSIPPI DELEGATION IN CONGRESS. *Harper's Weekly,* February 2, 1861, p. 65. Montage of portraits of the Mississippi delegation. 10⅞" × 9⅛". See page 51.

107. THE LATE REV. DR. MURRAY. *Harper's Weekly,* February 23, 1861, p. 117. Portrait. 5⅝" × 6¾". Not shown.

108. THE INAUGURAL PROCESSION AT WASHINGTON PASSING THE GATE OF THE CAPITOL GROUNDS. *Harper's Weekly,* March 16, 1861, p. 161. Large news illustration. 9⅛" × 10⅞". See page 54.

109. PRESIDENTS BUCHANAN AND LINCOLN ENTERING THE SENATE CHAMBER BEFORE THE INAUGURATION. *Harper's Weekly,* March 16, 1861, p. 165. News illustration. 9⅛" × 5⅞". See page 55.

110. THE INAUGURATION OF ABRAHAM LINCOLN AS PRESIDENT OF THE UNITED STATES, AT THE CAPITOL, WASHINGTON, MARCH 4, 1861. *Harper's Weekly,* March 16, 1861, pp. 168–169. News illustration. 20⅛" × 13¾". See page 56.

111. GENERAL THOMAS SWEARING IN THE VOLUNTEERS CALLED INTO THE SERVICE OF THE UNITED STATES AT WASHINGTON, D. C. *Harper's Weekly,* April 27, 1861, p. 257. News illustration. 9⅛" × 6⅜". See page 57.

112. GENERAL BEAUREGARD. *Harper's Weekly,* April 27, 1861, p. 269. Portrait. 5" × 6⅞". Not shown.

113. COLONEL WILSON, OF WILSON'S BRIGADE. *Harper's Weekly,* May 11, 1861, p. 289. Portrait. 5⅞" × 9⅛". Not shown.

114. THE SEVENTY-NINTH REGIMENT (HIGHLANDERS) NEW YORK STATE MILITIA. *Harper's Weekly,* May 25, 1861, p. 329. Scene showing the passing of soldiers dressed

in Scottish style, with plaids and bagpipes. 13⅞″ × 9¼″. See page 58.

115. THE ADVANCE GUARD OF THE GRAND ARMY OF THE UNITED STATES CROSSING THE LONG BRIDGE OVER THE POTOMAC, AT 2 A.M. ON MAY 24, 1861. *Harper's Weekly*, June 8, 1861, p. 356. 14″ × 9⅛″. News illustration. See page 59.

116. THE WAR-MAKING HAVELOCKS FOR THE VOLUNTEERS. *Harper's Weekly*, June 29, 1861, p. 401. Women make decorations for uniforms. 9¼″ × 10⅞″. See page 60.

117. CREW OF THE UNITED STATES STEAM-SLOOP "COLORADO," SHIPPED AT BOSTON, JUNE, 1861. *Harper's Weekly*, July 13, 1861, p. 439. Crew lined up on deck of ship to pose for artist. 13¾″ × 9¼″. See page 61.

118. FILLING CARTRIDGES AT THE UNITED STATES ARSENAL, AT WATERTOWN, MASSACHUSETTS. *Harper's Weekly*, July 20, 1861, p. 449. People depicted busy at work for war effort. 9¼″ × 10⅞″. See page 62.

119. FLAG-OFFICER STRINGHAM. *Harper's Weekly*, September 14, 1861, p. 577. Portrait. 4⅜″ × 4⅞″. Not shown.

120. THE SONGS OF THE WAR. *Harper's Weekly*, November 23, 1861, pp. 744–745. Montage depicting popular songs of the time. 20″ × 14″. See page 63.

121. A BIVOUAC FIRE ON THE POTOMAC. *Harper's Weekly*, December 21, 1861, pp. 808–809. Soldiers sit about fire as Negro dances for their entertainment. 20¼″ × 13¾″. See page 64.

122. GREAT FAIR GIVEN AT THE CITY ASSEMBLY ROOMS, NEW YORK, DECEMBER, 1861, IN AID OF THE CITY POOR. *Harper's Weekly*, December 28, 1861, pp. 824–825. Crowded scene of people among booths looking and purchasing wares. 20⅛″ × 13⅜″. See page 65.

123. CHRISTMAS BOXES IN CAMP—CHRISTMAS, 1861. *Harper's Weekly*, January 4, 1862, p. 1. Soldiers before tent open a crate to bring forth gifts of socks, etc. 9⅛″ × 10⅞″. See page 66.

124. THE SKATING SEASON—1862. *Harper's Weekly*, January 18, 1862, p. 44. Winter sport-scene. 13⅝″ × 9″. See page 67.

125. OUR ARMY BEFORE YORKTOWN, VIRGINIA. *Harper's Weekly*, May 3, 1862, pp. 280–281. Seven sketches of army maneuvers, but unsigned by either Homer or A. R. Waud, who both worked on the art. 20¾″ × 13¾″. See page 68.

126. REBELS OUTSIDE THEIR WORKS AT YORKTOWN RECONNOITRING [sic] WITH DARK LANTERNS. *Harper's Weekly*, May 17, 1862, p. 305. Night scene showing troops using hidden lamps to find lay of land. 9¼″ × 10⅞″. See page 70.

127. THE UNION CAVALRY AND ARTILLERY STARTING IN PURSUIT OF THE REBELS UP THE YORKTOWN TURNPIKE. *Harper's Weekly*, May 17, 1862, p. 308. News illustration. 13¾″ × 9¼″. See page 69.

128. CHARGE OF THE FIRST MASSACHUSETTS REGIMENT ON A REBEL RIFLE PIT NEAR YORKTOWN. *Harper's Weekly*, May 17, 1862, p. 309. News illustration. 9⅛″ × 6⅞″. See page 71.

129. THE ARMY OF THE POTOMAC—OUR OUTLYING PICKET IN THE WOODS. *Harper's Weekly*, June 7, 1862, p. 359. Soldiers lying in wait for attack in the woods. 9¼″ × 6⅞″. See page 72.

130. NEWS FROM THE WAR. *Harper's Weekly*, June 14, 1862, pp. 376–377. Montage of sketches showing the various ways persons received news of the war, and their reactions to it. 20¼″ × 13¼″. See page 73.

131. THE WAR FOR THE UNION, 1862—A CAVALRY CHARGE. *Harper's Weekly*, July 5, 1862, pp. 424–425. News illustration showing action of mounted attack on rebels. 20⅝″ × 13½″. See page 74.

132. THE SURGEON AT WORK AT THE REAR DURING AN ENGAGEMENT. *Harper's Weekly*, July 12, 1862, p. 436. Doctors taking care of the wounded at the front. 13¾″ × 9⅛″. See page 75.

133. THE WAR FOR THE UNION, 1862—A BAYONET CHARGE. *Harper's Weekly*, July 12, 1862, pp. 440–441. News illustration. 20⅝″ × 13⅝″. See page 76.

134. OUR WOMEN AND THE WAR. *Harper's Weekly*, September 6, 1862, pp. 568–569. Montage showing women busy with duties necessary to the war effort. 20⅜″ × 13⅝″. See page 77.

135. THE ARMY OF THE POTOMAC—A SHARP-SHOOTER ON PICKET DUTY. *Harper's Weekly*, November 15, 1862, p. 724. War scene of single soldier poised to shoot while in tree. Used as subject of Homer's first painting to be publicly exhibited. 13¾″ × 9⅛″. See page 78.

136. THANKSGIVING IN CAMP. *Harper's Weekly*, November 29, 1862, p. 764. Soldiers eat during pause in battle. 13¾″ × 9⅛″. See page 79.

137. A SHELL IN THE REBEL TRENCHES. *Harper's Weekly*, January 17, 1863, p. 36. Negroes frightened by a shell that exploded nearby in Rebel war area. 13¾″ × 9⅛″. See page 80.

138. WINTER-QUARTERS IN CAMP—THE INSIDE OF A HUT. *Harper's Weekly*, January 24, 1863, p. 52. Interior of stable-like area showing soldiers sleeping or at rest. 13⅞″ × 9⅛″. See page 81.

139. PAY-DAY IN THE ARMY OF THE POTOMAC. *Harper's Weekly*, February 28, 1863, pp. 136–137. Montage showing activities of soldiers off duty. 20½″ × 13⅝″. See page 82.

140. THE APPROACH OF THE BRITISH PIRATE "ALABAMA." *Harper's Weekly*, April 25, 1863, p. 268. Passengers on deck look at approaching ship. 9⅛″ × 13¾″. See page 84.

141. GREAT SUMTER MEETING IN UNION SQUARE, NEW YORK, APRIL 11, 1863. *Harper's Weekly*, April 25, 1863, p. 260. Public-gathering scene. 9⅛″ × 13¾″. Not shown.

142. HOME FROM THE WAR. *Harper's Weekly*, June 13, 1863, p. 381. Veterans being greeted by wives and families. 14″ × 9¼″. See page 83.

143. THE RUSSIAN BALL—IN THE SUPPER ROOM. *Harper's Weekly*, November 21, 1863, p. 737. Dance scene of social event. 9⅛″ × 10¾″. See page 85.

144. THE GREAT RUSSIAN BALL AT THE ACADEMY OF MUSIC, NOVEMBER 5, 1863. *Harper's Weekly*, November 21, 1863, pp. 744–745. Large-scale ballroom dance-scene. 20⅜″ × 13⅛″. See page 86.

145. HALT OF A WAGON TRAIN. *Harper's Weekly*, February 6, 1864, pp. 88–89. Night scene as wagon train pauses in journey. 20¼″ × 13⅜″. See page 87.

146. "ANY THING FOR ME, IF YOU PLEASE?"—POST OFFICE OF THE BROOKLYN FAIR IN AID OF THE SANITARY COMMISSION. *Harper's Weekly*, March 5, 1864, p. 156. Girl asking for mail at post-office window. 9⅛″ × 13⅝″. See page 88.

147. FLORAL DEPARTMENT OF THE GREAT FAIR. *Harper's Weekly*, April 16, 1864, p. 241. Indoor activity around floral displays. 9⅛″ × 10⅞″. See page 89.

148. ARMY OF THE POTOMAC—SLEEPING ON THEIR ARMS. *Harper's Weekly*, May 28, 1864, pp. 344–345. Soldiers sleep in fields on their guns. 20⅝″ × 13¾″. See page 90.

149. THANKSGIVING-DAY IN THE ARMY—AFTER DINNER: THE WISH-BONE. *Harper's Weekly*, December 3, 1864, p. 780. Two soldiers outdoors by fence, about to make a wish on turkey wishbone. 13⅞″ × 9¼″. See page 91.

150. THE COLD EMBRACE—"HE SEES THE RIGID FEATURES, THE MARBLE ARMS, THE HANDS CROSSED ON THE COLD BOSOM." *Frank Leslie's Chimney Corner*, June 24, 1865, p. 49. Story illustration: artist with sketch pad is seen lifting sheet to look at body of dead woman pulled from the sea. 6⅝″ × 8⅜″.

151. HOLIDAY IN CAMP—SOLDIERS PLAYING "FOOT-BALL." *Harper's Weekly*, July 15, 1865, p. 444. Union soldiers relax at a game of soccer. 13¾″ × 9¼″. See page 92.

152. OUR WATERING-PLACES—THE EMPTY SLEEVE AT NEWPORT. *Harper's Weekly*, August 26, 1865, p. 532. Woman in foreground drives carriage as veteran with one arm rides with her along the beach. 13¾″ × 9¼″. See page 93.

153. OUR WATERING-PLACES—HORSE-RACING AT SARATOGA. *Harper's Weekly*, August 26, 1865, p. 533. People gathered at racetrack to view the racing. 13¾″ × 9⅛″. See page 94.

154. LOOKING AT THE ECLIPSE. *Frank Leslie's Chimney Corner*, December 16, 1865, p. 37. Man and three women on a roof watch the eclipse through pieces of smoked glass. 9¼″ × 10¾″. Not shown.

155. THANKSGIVING DAY—HANGING UP THE MUSKET. *Frank Leslie's Illustrated News Paper*, December 23, 1865, p. 216. Man places a musket over mantel as wife watches him. 9⅛″ × 14⅛″. See page 95.

156. THANKSGIVING DAY—THE CHURCH PORCH. *Frank Leslie's Illustrated News Paper,* December 23, 1865, p. 217. Women and men—one an amputee—leave church. 9⅛" × 13⅞". See page 96.

157. OUR NATIONAL WINTER EXERCISE—SKATING. *Frank Leslie's Illustrated News Paper,* January 13, 1866, pp. 264–265. Two women skate at left, while in center woman is sprawled face forward on ice. 20½" × 14". Not shown.

158. THE BRIGHT SIDE. *Our Young Folks,* July, 1866, p. 396. Negroes rest at side of tent in sunshine. Based on a Homer painting. 3⅝" × 2¾". See page 97.

159. THE MIDNIGHT COAST. *The Riverside Magazine for Young People,* January, 1867, p. 14. Interesting night-scene showing 5 boys walking up a hill in the moonlight. 5⅜" × 5½". See page 99.

160. SWINGING ON A BIRCH TREE. *Our Young Folks,* June, 1867, Opposite p. 321. Boys seen sitting on branch of tree. 3⅝" × 5⅞". See page 98.

161. THE VETERAN IN A NEW FIELD. *Frank Leslie's Illustrated News Paper,* July 13, 1867, p. 268. Man with scythe cutting wheat. Based on painting. 6¼" × 4⅛". See page 97.

162. THE BIRD-CATCHERS. *Our Young Folks,* August, 1867, opposite p. 449. Three boys look into cage containing two birds. 5⅞" × 3⅝". See page 98.

163. A PARISIAN BALL—DANCING AT THE MABILLE, PARIS. *Harper's Weekly,* November 23, 1867, p. 744. Ballroom scene. 13¾" × 9⅛". See page 100.

164. A PARISIAN BALL—DANCING AT THE CASINO. *Harper's Weekly,* November 23, 1867, p. 745. Ballroom scene. 13¾" × 9⅛". See page 101.

165. HOMEWARD-BOUND. *Harper's Weekly,* December 21, 1867, pp. 808–809. Passengers stand on deck of ship in the wind. 20⅜" × 13⅞". See page 102.

166. ART-STUDENTS AND COPYISTS IN THE LOUVRE GALLERY, PARIS. *Harper's Weekly,* January 11, 1868, p. 25. Study showing students at art studies. 13¾" × 9". See page 103.

167. "WINTER"—A SKATING SCENE. *Harper's Weekly,* January 25, 1868, p. 52. Three girls skate while two women watch carefully over them. 13½" × 9". Not shown.

168. ST. VALENTINE'S—THE OLD STORY IN ALL LANDS. *Harper's Weekly,* February 22, 1868, p. 124. Montage showing couples around the world, with valentines and cupids all about. 9" × 13⅝". See page 104.

169. OPENING DAY IN NEW YORK. *Harper's Bazaar,* March 21, 1868, pp. 328–329. Montage showing women in various styles of the day. 20" × 13½". See page 105.

170. THE MORNING WALK—YOUNG LADIES' SCHOOL PROMENADING THE AVENUE. *Harper's Weekly,* March 28, 1868, p. 201. Girls in various fashions walk the avenue as men pretend not to notice them. 13⅝" × 9". Not shown.

171. "SHE TURNED HER FACE TO THE WINDOW." *The Galaxy,* May, 1868, opposite p. 581. Seated woman leans toward an open window. 7" × 4⅞". See page 106.

172. "YOU ARE REALLY PICTURESQUE, MY LOVE." *The Galaxy,* June, 1868, opposite p. 719. Man talks to young lady. 6⅞" × 4⅝". See page 107.

173. WATCHING THE CROWS. *Our Young Folks,* June, 1868, opposite p. 321. Boy with stick sits on fence watching crows in a field. 3⅝" × 5⅞". See page 108.

174. JESSIE REMAINED ALONE AT THE TABLE. *The Galaxy,* July, 1868, opposite p. 68. Girl holding billiard cue poised to shoot listens as other girls gossip in background. 6⅞" × 4⅞". Not shown.

175. THE STRAWBERRY BED. *Our Young Folks,* July, 1868, opposite p. 385. Children gather strawberries. 5⅝" × 3⅝". Not shown.

176. THE FOURTH OF JULY IN TOMPKINS SQUARE, NEW YORK—"THE SOGERS ARE COMING!" *Harper's Bazaar,* July 11, 1868, p. 588. Small children in foreground watch fireworks as men play game in left background. 12¼" × 8⅛". See page 109.

177. FIRE-WORKS ON THE NIGHT OF THE FOURTH OF JULY. *Harper's Weekly,* July 11, 1868, p. 445. Night scene showing a crowd of people looking up to watch fireworks display. 13¾" × 9⅛". See page 110.

178. NEW ENGLAND FACTORY LIFE—BELL-TIME. *Harper's Weekly,* July 25, 1868, p. [illegible]. Large group of people leaving work. 12⅞" × 8¾". See page 111.

179. "ORRIN, MAKE HASTE, I AM PERISHING!" *The Galaxy,* August 1868, opposite p. 217. Girl holding onto post is sinking into pond. 6⅞" × 4⅝". Not shown.

180. GREEN APPLES. *Our Young Folks,* August, 1868, opposite p. 449. Boy watches another boy pull apples from a tree. 3⅝" × 5⅞". Not shown.

181. "I CANNOT! IT WOULD BE A SIN! A FEARFUL SIN!" *The Galaxy,* September, 1868, opposite p. 341. Man stands over a seated woman, who is crying. 4⅞" × 6⅞". Not shown.

182. BLUE BEARD TABLEAU. *Harper's Bazaar,* September 5, 1868, p. 717. (A) FATIMA ENTERS THE FORBIDDEN CLOSET. 4⅛" × 4⅛". (B) WHAT SHE SEES THERE. 8¼" × 3½". (C) DISPOSITION OF THE BODIES (INVISIBLE TO THE SPECTATORS). 4⅛" × 3⅞". Homer visits the theatre to show the public what a popular play is like and how effects are worked. See pages 112, 113.

183. "OUR NEXT PRESIDENT." *Harper's Weekly,* October 31, 1868, p. 689. People raise their glasses to toast incoming President, whose picture is seen on the wall. 9⅛" × 10⅞". See page 114.

184. OUR MINISTER'S DONATION PARTY. *Harper's Bazaar,* December 19, 1868, p. 952. Parlor scene showing members of congregation rushing into room with gifts for minister and his family. 13¾" × 9¼". Not shown.

185. WAITING FOR CALLS ON NEW-YEAR'S DAY. *Harper's Bazaar,* January 2, 1869, p. 9. Young ladies, some seated, some at window of parlor, waiting for guests. 13¾" × 9". See page 115.

186. CHRISTMAS BELLES. *Harper's Weekly,* January 2, 1869, p. 8. Lovely ladies seated in sleigh being driven through country. 13⅝" × 9$\frac{1}{16}$". See page 116.

187. THE NEW YEAR—1869. *Harper's Weekly,* January 9, 1869, p. 20. A young boy—the New Year—bursts through a paper hoop on his bicycle. 13¾" × 9". See page 117.

188. WINTER AT SEA—TAKING IN SAIL OFF THE COAST. *Harper's Weekly,* January 16, 1869, p. 40. Sailors fold up sail while balancing on a spar high above the deck. 12⅞" × 8⅞". See page 118.

189. JURORS LISTENING TO COUNSEL, SUPREME COURT, NEW CITY HALL, NEW YORK. *Harper's Weekly,* February 20, 1969, p. 120. Courtroom scene. 13⅝" × 9". See page 119.

190. "HI! H-O-O-O! HE DONE COME. JUMBOLORO TELL YOU FUST." *The Galaxy,* June, 1869, opposite p. 823. Negro in anxious state rushes toward woman on porch. 4⅞" × 6⅞". See page 120.

191. "ALL IN THE GAY AND GOLDEN WEATHER." *Appleton's Journal of Literature, Science, and Art,* June 16, 1869, p. 321. Man and woman in boat relax in lovely setting. 6½" × 5½". See page 121.

192. THE ARTIST IN THE COUNTRY. *Appleton's Journal of Literature, Science, and Art,* June 19, 1869, p. 353. Artist sits under umbrella in country in front of easel while woman looks over his shoulder. 6⅝" × 6¼". See page 122.

193. SUMMER IN THE COUNTRY. *Appleton's Journal of Literature, Science, and Art,* July 10, 1869, p. 465. Young ladies play croquet in country scene. 6½" × 4½". See page 123.

194. THE SUMMIT OF MOUNT WASHINGTON. *Harper's Weekly,* July 10, 1869, p. 441. Large panorama showing persons on horseback amid the mountains and gorges. 9" × 13¾". Not shown.

195. ON THE ROAD TO LAKE GEORGE. *Appleton's Journal of Literature, Science, and Art,* July 24, 1869, p. 513. Country children in foreground watch elegantly dressed people in coach pass by them. 6⅝" × 6⅛". See page 124.

196. WHAT SHALLL WE DO NEXT? *Harper's Bazaar,* July 31, 1869, p. 488. Women rest after a game of croquet. 13¾" × 9⅛". See page 125.

197. THE LAST LOAD. *Appleton's Journal of Literature, Science, and Art,* August 7, 1869, p. 592. Three persons stand and look at a recently mowed hayfield. 6½" × 4½". See page 126.

198. THE PICNIC EXCURSION. *Appleton's Journal of Literature, Science, and Art,* August 14, 1869, p. 624. People in wagons wait for picnic trip to begin. 9⅛" × 6½". See page 127.

199. THE BEACH AT LONG BRANCH. *Appleton's Journal of Literature, Science, and Art,* August 21, 1869, Supplement. Fully dressed women and men head toward the beach, where figures are seen in the water in the background. 19⅜" × 13". See page 128.

200. At the Spring: Saratoga. *Hearth and Home,* August 28, 1869, p. 561. Elegantly dressed people stand about in area near spa. 8½″ × 9⅛″. See page 129.
201. "Come!" *The Galaxy,* September, 1869, opposite page 293. An eager young man waves to a young woman through a window. 6⅞″ × 4¾″. See page 130.
202. The Straw Ride. *Harper's Bazaar,* September 25, 1869, p. 620. Persons seen seated amid hay in back of wagon. 13⅞″ × 9⅛″. See page 131.
203. "I Call Them My Children—to Myself, Susan." *The Galaxy,* October, 1869, opposite p. 437. Elderly minister-type person points out flowers to young woman by his side. 6⅞″ × 4½″. See page 132.
204. The Fishing Party. *Appleton's Journal of Literature, Science, and Art,* October 2, 1869, Supplement. Women and men seen near stream or fishing in it. 13¾″ × 9″. See page 134.
205. Weary and Dissatisfied with Everything. *The Galaxy,* November, 1869, opposite p. 581. Tired, disheveled woman seen seated by table. 4⅝″ × 7″. See page 133.
206. The Playmates. *Our Young Folks,* November, 1869, opposite p. 760. Boy and girl standing in a field. 3⅝″ × 3⅝″. See page 135.
207. In Came a Storm of Wind, Rain and Spray—and Portia. *The Galaxy,* December, 1869, opposite p. 725. Woman soaked to skin comes rushing into room through glass door as another woman watches her. 4⅜″ × 6½″. See page 136.
208. George Blake's Letter. *The Galaxy,* January, 1870, frontispiece. Young woman reads a letter in front of a window. 4½″ × 6½″. See page 137.
209. Another Year by the Old Clock. *Harper's Bazaar,* January 1, 1870, p. 1. Elderly couple seated in parlor, she asleep, and he watching clock turn toward midnight. 11″ × 15½″. Not shown.
210. 1860–1870. *Harper's Weekly,* January 8, 1870, pp. 24–25. Montage panels showing events of past decade, including the war and attempts at integration. 20⅜″ × 13″. See page 138.
211. Tenth Commandment. *Harper's Weekly,* March 12, 1870, p. 161. Women seen at church, praying, amid other scenes. 9″ × 10½″. See page 139.
212. Danger Ahead. *Appleton's Journal of Literature, Science, and Art,* April 30, 1870, p. 477. Night scene: train speeds over tracks and boy leans to look out ahead. 6½″ × 6⅛″. See page 140.
213. Spring Farm Work—Grafting. *Harper's Weekly,* April 30, 1870, p. 276. Men at work in arbor area of farm. 9⅛″ × 6⅞″. See page 141.
214. Spring Blossoms. *Harper's Weekly,* May 21, 1870, p. 328. Woman seated and watching children play with toy boat in water trough nearby. 13⅞″ × 9⅛″. See page 142.
215. The Dinner Horn. *Harper's Weekly,* June 11, 1870, p. 377. Woman on porch blows horn to call in family. 9″ × 13¾″. See page 143.
216. A Quiet Day in the Woods. *Appleton's Journal of Literature, Science, and Art,* June 25, 1870, p. 701. Man and woman seated on ground in shadowy woods. 6½″ × 6⅛″. See page 144.
217. The Coolest Spot in New England—Summit of Mount Washington. *Harper's Bazaar.* July 23, 1870, p. 473. Resort visitors stand or sit atop a bluff, looking out on the countryside about them as breeze blows over them. 9⅛″ × 13¾″. See page 145.
218. High Tide. *Every Saturday,* August 6, 1870, p. 504. Three women in bathing costume at water's edge. 11¾″ × 8⅞″. See page 146.
219. Low Tide. *Every Saturday,* August 6, 1870, p. 505. Young girls in street clothes and children in background in beach clothes all play on the beach. 11¾″ × 8⅞″. See page 147.
220. On the Bluff at Long Branch, at the Bathing Hour. *Harper's Weekly,* August 6, 1870, p. 504. Ladies in wind-tossed costumes look down from bluff at crowded beach below. 13⅝″ × 8⅞″. See page 148.
221. The Robin's Note. *Every Saturday,* August 20, 1870, p. 529. Woman seated in string hammock listens to robin's call. 8⅞″ × 9″. See page 149.
222. On the Beach at Long Branch. *Harper's Bazaar,* September 3, 1870, p. 569. Closeup of three young women chatting as they drive in a carriage, with the beach in the background. 13¾″ × 9″. Not shown.
223. Chestnutting. *Every Saturday,* October 29, 1870, p. 700. Children hold sheet spread out beneath chestnut tree as boy in tree knocks the nuts off the branches. 8⅞″ × 11¾″. See page 150.
224. Trapping in the Adirondacks. *Every Saturday,* December 24, 1870, p. 849. Two hunters seated in a canoe coming back with game caught in traps. 11⅝″ × 8⅞″. See page 151.
225. A Winter-Morning—Shovelling Out. *Every Saturday,* January 14, 1871, p. 32. Two men and a boy shovel out from huge fall of snow, as woman feeds birds in background. 11¾″ × 8⅞″. See page 152.
226. Deer-Stalking in the Adirondacks in Winter. *Every Saturday,* January 21, 1871, p. 57. Two men in foreground aim at deer in background being chased by dogs. 11⅝″ × 8⅞″. See page 153.
227. Lumbering in Winter. *Every Saturday,* January 28, 1871, p. 89. Two men cut down trees and chop them up for firewood. 8⅞″ × 11⅝″. See page 154.
228. Cutting a Figure. *Every Saturday,* February 4, 1871, pp. 116–117. Beautiful woman in foreground seen cutting a figure eight while others skate along shore behind her. 18⅝″ × 11$\frac{11}{16}$″. See pages 156–157.
229. A Country Store—Getting Weighed. *Every Saturday,* March 25, 1871, p. 272. Group of women stand around interior of dark store waiting to be weighed by a man on store scales. 11⅝″ × 8⅞″. See page 155.
230. At Sea—Signalling a Passing Steamer. *Every Saturday,* April 8, 1871, p. 321. Dark, stormy scene, with lights being used to send messages to other ships. 11⅝″ × 8¾″. See page 158.
231. Bathing at Long Branch—"Oh, Ain't It Cold!" *Every Saturday,* August 26, 1871, p. 213. Three women in bathing costumes stand amid the waves. 11¾″ × 9⅛″. See page 159.
232. Making Hay. *Harper's Weekly,* July 6, 1872, p. 529. Children with water bucket watch as two men scythe hay in background. 13⅞″ × 9⅛″. See page 160.
233. On the Beach—Two Are Company, Three Are None. *Harper's Weekly,* August 17, 1872, p. 636. Woman with parasol looks down at young couple seated by grounded boat on beach. 13¾″ × 9⅛″. See page 161.
234. Under the Falls, Catskill Mountains. *Harper's Weekly,* September 14, 1872, p. 721. Two women in foreground look at figures near waterfall in background. 13⅞″ × 9⅛″. See page 162.
235. The Wreck of the "Atlantic"—Cast Up By The Sea. *Harper's Weekly,* April 26, 1873, p. 345. Grim scene: passing man finds the dead body of woman in underclothes washed up on beach. 13¾″ × 9⅛″. See page 163.
236. The Noon Recess. *Harper's Weekly,* June 28, 1873, p. 549. Bad boy and bored teacher sit in dark classroom as children are seen, through the windows, playing outside. 13⅝″ × 9⅛″. See page 164.
237. The Bathers. *Harper's Weekly,* August 16, 1873, p. 668. Two lovely ladies wave to figure in background amid other figures on beach. 9¼″ × 13¾″. See page 165.
238. The Nooning. *Harper's Weekly,* August 16, 1873, p. 725. Three boys with dog rest in shade as household activities go on about them. 13¾″ × 9″. See page 166.
239. Sea-Side Sketches—A Clam-Bake. *Harper's Weekly,* August 23, 1873, p. 740. Barefoot boys on rocks bring driftwood and clams to pit already set for the clam-bake. 14″ × 9¼″. See page 167.
240. "Snap-the-Whip." *Harper's Weekly,* September 20, 1873, pp. 824–825. Country boys, all linked together by arms, play exciting game in schoolyard. 12¾″ × 8⅜″. See page 168.
241. Gloucester Harbor. *Harper's Weekly,* September 27, 1873, p. 844. Boys afloat on water in two boats watch the harbor activity. 14″ × 9⅜″. See page 169.
242. Ship-Building, Gloucester Harbor. *Harper's Weekly,* October 11, 1873, p. 900. Little boys copy older men by making small boats in foreground as men work on huge ship which dominates the background. 13¾″ × 9⅜″. See page 170.
243. "Dad's Coming!" *Harper's Weekly,* November 1, 1873, p. 969. Mother, baby, and young boy look out at sea to watch for return of father as boats come into view. 13½″ × 9¼″. See page 171.

244. THE LAST DAYS OF HARVEST. *Harper's Weekly,* December 6, 1873, p. 1092. Two boys shuck corn in foreground as pumpkins are being pitched into wagons behind them. 13⅜" × 9¼". See page 172.
245. THE MORNING BELL. *Harper's Weekly,* December 13, 1873, p. 1116. Bell calls workers in from surrounding area. 13½" × 9⅛". See page 173.
246. STATION-HOUSE LODGERS. *Harper's Weekly,* February 7, 1874, p. 132. Police look through door in background to view a number of men asleep on floor in various poses. 13½" × 9⅛". See page 174.
247. WATCH-TOWER, CORNER OF SPRING AND VARICK STREETS, NEW YORK. *Harper's Weekly,* February 28, 1874, p. 196. (A) WATCHMAN. 9⅛" × 5½". (B) THE TOWER. 2" × 8". (C) THE BELL. 4⅞" × 8". (D) NINE O'CLOCK BELL. 2¼" × 4". (E) A FIRE. 1⅞" × 3⅜". Homer cleverly integrated all five pictures to show various views and activities. See page 175.
248. THE CHINESE IN NEW YORK—SCENE IN A BAXTER STREET CLUB-HOUSE. *Harper's Weekly,* March 7, 1874, p. 212. Interior scene showing smoky room full of Chinese men smoking long pipes and looking dreamy. 9⅛" × 10⅞". See page 176.
249. NEW YORK CHARITIES—ST. BARNABAS HOUSE, 304 MULBERRY STREET. *Harper's Weekly,* April 18, 1874, p. 336. Montage of scenes showing women and their charity activities at the home. 13⅜" × 9⅛". See page 177.
250. RAID ON A SAND-SWALLOW COLONY—"HOW MANY EGGS?" *Harper's Weekly,* June 13, 1874, p. 496. Boys seen entering nesting area of the swallows in the dunes. 9⅛" × 13⅜". See page 178.
251. GATHERING BERRIES. *Harper's Weekly,* July 11, 1874, p. 584. Childern gather berries in field. 13½" × 9⅛". See page 179.
252. ON THE BEACH AT LONG BRANCH—THE CHILDREN'S HOUR. *Harper's Weekly,* August 15, 1874, p. 672. Mothers and nurses with tots seen on the beach. 13⅝" × 9¼". See page 180.
253. WAITING FOR A BITE. *Harper's Weekly,* August 22, 1874, p. 693. Three boys sit on fallen tree in woods with their lines in the water waiting for fish to bite. 13¾" × 9⅛". See page 181.
254. SEESAW—GLOUCESTER, MASSACHUSETTS. *Harper's Weekly,* September 12, 1874, p. 757. Children playing on the beach, with boys in direct center on a seesaw. 13¾" × 9⅛". See page 182.
255. FLIRTING ON THE SEA-SHORE AND ON THE MEADOW. *Harper's Weekly,* September 19, 1874, p. 780. (A) Sailor and lady sit looking at a moonlit sea. 13½" × 5". (B) Two boys lying on their stomachs in a sunlit meadow face a pretty girl seated opposite them. 13½" × 4⅛". See page 183.
256. CAMPING OUT IN THE ADIRONDACK MOUNTAINS. *Harper's Weekly,* November 7, 1874, p. 920. Guide and camper sit among assorted equipment on a lake shore. 13¾" × 9⅛". See page 184.
257. THE BATTLE OF BUNKER HILL—WATCHING THE FIGHT FROM COPP'S HILL, IN BOSTON. *Harper's Weekly,* June 26, 1875, p. 517. Historical drawing done for magazine article. 13⅝" × 9⅛". See frontispiece.
258. THE FAMILY RECORD. *Harper's Bazaar,* August 28, 1875, p. 561. Father and mother enter the birth of their child, nearby in cradle, in the family Bible. 8⅛" × 12". See page 185.
259. THE SOWER. *Scribner's Monthly,* August, 1878, p. 515. Farm scene. 5" × 2⅞". Not shown.
260. PUMPKINS AMONG THE CORN. *Scribner's Monthly,* August, 1878, p. 520. Farm scene. 5" × 3¼". Not shown.
261. A LITTORAL LIFE. *Scribner's Monthly,* January, 1879, p. 403. Flirtation on the beach. 2¾" × 2⅝". Not shown.
262. GATHERING WILD BLACKBERRIES. *Scribner's Monthly,* April, 1880, p. 806. Girls pick berries in a field. [illegible]. Not shown.
263. SPRING LAMB. *Scribner's Monthly,* June, 1880, p. 161. Lambs among ewes at springtime. 4⅝" × 4". Not shown.
264. "BOSSY." *The Art Interchange,* December 22, 1880, p. 129. Sketch of man and calf, with chickens flocking nearby. 8⅝" × 6⅞". Not shown.
265. BOB: "HELLO! WHAT'S UP NOW? ARE YOUR BABIES IN HERE?" *St. Nicholas,* July, 1881, p. 664. Boy stops cutting grain in field when he notices birds making a fuss over an area near him. 5¼" × 3½". See page 186.

Illustrations 266–270 were not done by Homer for magazine publication but were used to illustrate an article on him.

266. A CHARCOAL SKETCH. *The Century Magazine,* November, 1883, p. 13. Men struggle to beach a longboat. 5¼" × 3⅜". See page 187.
267. "LOOKING OVER THE CLIFF. *The Century Magazine,* November, 1883, p. 16. Two women find comfort in holding hands as they look down from a cliff. 4¾" × 6⅞". See page 188.
268. LISTENING TO THE VOICE FROM THE CLIFFS. *The Century Magazine,* November, 1883, p. 18. Three women, one with a net and two with baskets, stop and listen to the sound of the wind and surf coming from the cliff behind them. 5⅛" × 3¾". See page 189.
269. "INSIDE THE BAR." *The Century Magazine,* November, 1883, p. 20. Detail illustration showing center of painting in which a woman is standing on the shore with a basket in her hands as the winds whip about her. 4⅞" × 7⅜". See page 190.
270. OUTLINE OF "INSIDE THE BAR." *The Century Magazine,* November, 1883, p. 21. Outline drawing showing woman of Illustration 269 at center, while at left boats lift sails, and at right, boat heads out to sea with sails still lowered. 3½" × 2". Not shown.
271. RUSH'S LANCERS. FRANKLIN'S ADVANCE SCOUTS. *The Century Magazine,* May, 1886, p. 136. Historical illustration based on a Homer sketch from the war. 5⅛" × 3⅛". See page 191.

Illustrations 272–280 are based on Homer's watercolor studies of Nassau, and their titles amply describe each illustration.

272. A GROUP OF PALMS. *The Century Magazine,* February, 1887, p. 500. 2⁷⁄₁₆" × 3". See page 192.
273. A HURRICANE. *The Century Magazine,* February, 1887, p. 501. 2½" × 1⅜". See page 192.
274. GROWING HEMP. *The Century Magazine,* February, 1887, p. 501. 2½" × 1⅜". See page 192.
275. ON ABACO ISLAND. *The Century Magazine,* February, 1887, p. 501. 2½" × 1¾". See page 193.
276. THE FLOWER-SELLER. *The Century Magazine,* February, 1887, p. 501. 2½" × 1¾". See page 193.
277. CONCH DIVERS. *The Century Magazine,* February, 1887, p. 502. 5¼" × 3¾". See page 194.
278. A PEDDLER. *The Century Magazine,* February, 1887, p. 503. 1¾" × 1¾". Not shown.
279. A NASSAU GATEWAY. *The Century Magazine,* February, 1887, p. 503. 1¾" × 1¾". Not shown.
280. SHARK-FISHING. *The Century Magazine,* February, 1887, p. 504. 5¼" × 3¾". See page 195.
281. SOME MEN OF THE SECOND CORPS WHO FOUGHT AT PETERSBURG. *The Century Magazine,* September, 1887, p. 783. Heads of the men, all wearing caps. 5¼" × 1¾". Not shown.
282. TWO OF SHERIDAN'S SCOUTS. *The Century Magazine,* November, 1887. Two scouts on horseback. 4½" × 4". See page 196.
283. PRESIDENT LINCOLN, GENERAL GRANT, AND TAD LINCOLN AT A RAILWAY STATION. *The Century Magazine,* November, 1887, p. 134. Sketch done from life. 3" × 2⅞". See page 197.
284. THE BAGGAGE GUARD. *The Century Magazine,* February, 1888, p. 324. Soldiers defending a mule train. 5¼" × 1¾". See page 196.